Charming or Chilling? Signs to Notice When You Are Approached by the Criminal Mind

Recognizing Manipulative Behaviors Before They Become a Part of Your Life

Iraklis Vogiatzidakis & Maraki

Table of Contents

Introduction

In a world where seeking human connection is both essential and deeply vulnerable, we often don't like to think about the fact that there may be criminals and dark characters among us. Yet, the most insidious and dangerous individuals we might encounter as we build relationships and enter into a community often remain hidden in plain sight—smooth talkers who seem well-meaning.

In this book, we will delve into the chilling traits, behaviors, and warning signs of antisocial personalities—individuals whose deceptive prowess serves both as a means of survival and as a weapon against the vulnerable.

Sociopaths, psychopaths, and those with antisocial personality disorder (ASPD) possess a dangerous ability to deceive, control, and even destroy lives, often without the victim realizing the full extent of their manipulation until it is far too late. These individuals are frighteningly common. It is in these moments—when trust has been betrayed, when one feels emotionally or even physically battered—that the need to understand the nature of these individuals becomes not just important but urgent.

This book is designed to illuminate the inner workings of antisocial personalities and criminal minds and equip you with the wisdom to recognize the signs you have encountered one of these individuals before their damage becomes irreparable.

By gaining a deeper understanding of the science and psychology behind sociopathy and psychopathy, we will not only better grasp the complex patterns that govern these individuals' behavior, but we will also explore the manipulation strategies they employ. This will provide us with a useful window into recognizing the subtle cues that mark their presence and, most importantly, equip you with the tools you need to protect yourself and your loved ones from dangerous individuals.

Through this exploration, you will gain the detailed knowledge necessary to see beyond the surface of common interactions, to recognize the early warning signs of potential harm that often go unnoticed, and to build a shield of protection through that knowledge. Empowered with this awareness, you may start to notice more dark characters in your everyday experiences, which may initially feel alarming. However, you will also know that you are no longer at the mercy of those who seek to use and control others for their own gain.

The ultimate goal is to transform your understanding of human behavior, fortify your emotional defenses, and navigate a world fraught with manipulation and deceit with confidence and clarity.

Chapter 1:

Behind the Mask—Unveiling the Antisocial Personality

Have you ever encountered someone who acts impulsively, without concern for others, or seems to lack empathy altogether? Maybe you've wondered why some people consistently act destructively, break societal rules, and manipulate those around them. These behaviors can be perplexing, especially when they disrupt your life or create chaos in your community.

What drives these individuals to act seemingly without remorse? It's estimated that between 1-4% of the general population has something called antisocial personality disorder (ASPD), a mental health condition marked by consistent disregard for others, among other traits (*Antisocial Personality Disorder: Symptoms & Treatment*, 2017).

Gaining a better understanding of this condition can provide insight into these troubling patterns, as well as provide tools to safeguard against their impact. In this chapter, we will delve into some of this disorder's key characteristics and traits, exploring how they shape behavior and influence social interactions.

A Masterclass in Manipulation

Denise hadn't been looking for romance that night. She was simply waiting at an upscale bar for a friend when she noticed him watching her. Lucas was polished and confident—his gaze held just the right amount of intensity. When he finally approached, his presence felt effortless, as though they were meant to meet, the conversation easy, and his compliments perfectly timed. By the time her friend arrived, Lucas had already charmed his way into their evening.

When the bill came, he didn't reach for his wallet. Somehow, Denise and her friend ended up splitting it while Lucas continued spinning his spell. It should have been a red flag, but instead, she barely noticed, lost in his charm.

As they stepped out onto the street, Lucas offered to walk her home. It wasn't a request but a natural extension of the evening, as if they had already established an unspoken connection. Then, just before they reached her building, the tone shifted. His girlfriend had kicked him out that morning and he hadn't figured out where he was going that evening. Denise hesitated. She knew better than to invite a stranger into her home, but Lucas felt different. He had an expensive watch and well-tailored clothes—he clearly wasn't a drifter. And he made her feel special, chosen. So, against her instincts, she invited him in.

One night turned into a week. A week into a month. Lucas never left, but she didn't mind. She was happy to have his presence, and he showered her in praise and affection. It all felt so natural that when one day, he surprised her with an engagement ring, it didn't feel shocking, despite the growing concern of friends and family members.

Yet one thing was off. While he'd told her he was a day trader who worked out of a shared office downtown, Lucas never had money, and Denise found herself covering all the bills, nights out, and other expenses, with Lucas promising to repay her after a few big investments paid off. If she questioned him, he didn't get angry. Instead, he made her feel guilty—how could she doubt the honesty of a man who loved her so deeply? Often, he became even more affectionate, ensuring she never stayed upset for long.

The police came early one morning. Denise opened the door to find them standing there, asking for Lucas by name. She barely had time to process what was happening before they were cuffing him.

Fraud. Extortion. Years of deception. While Lucas had been telling Denise he loved her, he had been systematically conning other women—pressuring them for money, forging documents, spinning endless lies.

Lucas wasn't just a liar; he was a skilled con man. His charm had never been true affection; it was a means to an end. Perhaps most insidious was that often he didn't steal. Instead, he convinced people to give, using a mix of flattery and deception. Lucas was a textbook case of antisocial personality disorder. His manipulation was subtle yet effective, ensuring that by the time his victims realized what had happened, they were already too deep to escape unscathed.

What Is Antisocial Personality Disorder?

Antisocial personality disorder (ASPD) is a mental health condition predominantly characterized by a persistent disregard for the rights and well-being of others. However, individuals with ASPD often also exhibit impulsivity, deceitfulness, irritability, and a striking lack of remorse for their actions. These traits conform to the standards established by psychological diagnostic criteria that we'll cover in more depth in the next section, but in summary, it's a pathological set of manipulative and harmful behaviors that can be identified through certain behavioral patterns.

Awareness of ASPD can empower us not only to be better able to identify potential harm but to proceed in our social interactions with greater caution and confidence. One key characteristic of ASPD is a compelling pattern of violating social norms in ways that are detrimental to others or one's community (American Psychiatric Association, 2013). Other key traits include:

- **Lack of Empathy:** They often dismiss or act callously toward others' feelings. For example, they may commit a crime without showing any regret or deceive a friend for personal gain.

- **Impulsivity:** They make reckless decisions—engaging in risky behaviors such as substance abuse or dangerous driving—without concern for consequences.

- **Chronic Deceit:** Lying and manipulation are common tools they use to achieve their goals, whether for financial gain, social leverage, or mere amusement.

- **Aggressiveness:** Some react with physical violence to minor provocations, while others employ long-term psychological manipulation to erode a victim's confidence and sense of reality.

These behaviors are not just occasional; they go beyond minor infractions or rebellious teenage acts to be consistent characteristics of one's overall personality. Someone with ASPD is likely to display a pervasive tendency to prioritize self-interest at any cost, sometimes dramatically so. For example, a person with ASPD might embezzle money from their employer, fully ignoring the legal and criminal consequences and justifying their actions as a way to enhance their own financial situation.

The Impact of Antisocial Personality Disorder on Relationships

Antisocial personality disorder's (ASPD) potential impact on relationships is severe. The often callous and harmful behaviors of a person with ASPD can be coupled with irritability and aggressiveness. For example, someone with ASPD might react with physical violence to a minor provocation, or they may engage in long-term manipulation, gradually eroding their victim's self-esteem. These behaviors can create long-lasting toxic impacts and recognizing them early can help potential victims protect themselves (Williams, 2023).

When in a relationship with someone with ASPD, unhealthy dynamics can become the norm, often trapping partners, friends, or family members in cycles of emotional manipulation and abuse. Individuals in relationships with someone who has ASPD may experience repeated betrayal and aggression, leading to loss of trust, confusion, and even isolation.

For example, a romantic partner might initially be drawn to the individual's charm and confidence, only to find themselves subjected to emotional blackmail and deceit later. Over time, these tactics can not only have external impacts but can also erode self-worth, leaving the victims feeling trapped and confused. This dynamic affects the immediate victims and can have a ripple effect, leading to strained relationships with others, loss of trust, and even isolation.

The impulsivity of those with antisocial personality disorder also often leads to risky decision-making that negatively affects both personal and professional relationships. Their compulsion to act without forethought often results in unsafe sex, substance abuse, and various forms of criminal activity.

In personal relationships, this impulsivity can result in unpredictable and hurtful actions that create instability and chaos. Again, understanding these traits and behaviors as part of a larger pattern better equips individuals and mental health practitioners to recognize early warning signs, potentially shielding them from harm.

DSM-V Criteria for Antisocial Personality Disorder

While we've begun to identify the traits of ASPD, to gain a more comprehensive understanding of its impacts, we should also take a closer look at its psychiatric foundations.

The fifth edition of the *Diagnostic and Statistical Manual of Mental Disorders* (DSM-V), the reference that sets the standard for diagnosing mental disorders, sets forth several specific criteria that define this condition. Understanding these criteria is useful for clinicians and anyone looking to grasp the complexity of ASPD and successfully mitigate its potential negative impacts.

According to the DSM-V, ASPD is characterized by "a pervasive pattern of disregard for, and violation of, the rights of others, beginning in childhood or early adolescence and continuing into adulthood" (American Psychiatric Association, 2013). The specific diagnostic criteria also include the following:

- **Failure to Conform to Social Norms:** Individuals with ASPD repeatedly engage in behaviors that are grounds for arrest, demonstrating a blatant disregard for laws and societal expectations.

- **Deception:** Chronic lying, use of aliases, and conning others for personal gain or pleasure are hallmarks of the disorder.

- **Impulsivity and Lack of Planning:** Those with ASPD often make spur-of-the-moment decisions without considering consequences, leading to unstable life patterns.

- **Irritability and Aggression**: Repeated physical altercations, assaults, or extreme verbal aggression are common traits.

- **Reckless Disregard for Safety**: A lack of concern for the well-being of oneself or others is frequently observed, leading to dangerous behaviors such as reckless driving or substance abuse.

- **Consistent Irresponsibility:** Individuals with ASPD often fail to sustain consistent work behavior or meet financial obligations, demonstrating chronic unreliability.

- **Lack of Remorse:** An absence of guilt or empathy is evident, as these individuals rationalize or trivialize the harm they inflict on others.

The specificity of these criteria serves as a guide to differentiating between troubling behaviors that may be a reaction to external circumstances compared to a formally diagnosed personality disorder. This can help to recognize whether someone is likely to be a source of persistent challenges and also allows mental health professionals to adequately attribute observed behaviors to ASPD and provide the most appropriate and impactful solutions.

A diagnosis of ASPD requires substantial evidence and a consistent pattern over time. For that reason, the individual must be at least 18 years old at the time of diagnosis. Additionally, there must be evidence of conduct disorder symptoms before the age of 15, such as aggression toward people or animals, destruction of property, deceitfulness, or serious violations of rules (American Psychiatric Association, 2013).

Differentiating Antisocial Personality Disorder From Other Mental Health Conditions

It's especially important to understand that a personality disorder such as ASPD is distinct from other mental health conditions that are considered behavioral disorders, such as mood disorders (e.g., depression, bipolar disorder) or psychotic disorders (e.g., schizophrenia). While many mental illnesses involve temporary or episodic disturbances in thought, emotion, or behavior, personality disorders are characterized by deeply ingrained, inflexible patterns of thinking and interacting with the world. These patterns are not temporary; they define how an individual consistently relates to others and functions in daily life.

Unlike conditions that may fluctuate or respond well to treatment, personality disorders—particularly ASPD—tend to be pervasive, resistant to change, and often lack the self-awareness that would prompt the individual to seek help (Fisher et al., 2024).

This distinction is essential when evaluating individuals with ASPD. They do not simply experience emotional distress or struggle with internal conflicts—they often fundamentally lack the capacity for empathy, guilt, or meaningful interpersonal connection, making them uniquely dangerous in both personal and societal contexts.

As such, the ethical considerations accompanying the diagnosis of ASPD are significant, as it involves attributing a label that might dramatically affect life trajectories. Clinicians are unlikely to diagnose a personality disorder without deep consideration, as these labels can impact social, legal, and personal spheres (Kaylor, 1999).

When Traits Don't Equal a Diagnosis

Personality disorders—especially ASPD—are complex and require a thorough clinical evaluation by trained professionals. Misusing the term to describe someone who is merely selfish, manipulative, or emotionally distant dilutes the severity of the disorder and can lead to stigma, misjudgments, and dehumanization. As such, it is important to understand that many people exhibit some traits associated with ASPD—such as dishonesty, impulsivity, or a disregard for rules—at various points in their lives, particularly in high-stress environments or during adolescence. However, these behaviors alone do not constitute a disorder.

For example, a ruthless business executive who bends ethical rules for financial gain may demonstrate antisocial qualities, but if they can form meaningful relationships, experience guilt, and adjust their behavior based on consequences, they do not meet the criteria for ASPD. Similarly, a rebellious teenager who shoplifts or lies to their parents is not necessarily on a path toward a lifelong disorder—many adolescents engage in risk-taking behavior that they later outgrow.

Recognizing a Pattern, Not an Episode

On the other hand, consider a woman in her mid-30s who has displayed recurring aggressive behavior and manipulative tendencies since her teenage years. Despite facing legal repercussions and a series of failed friendships and relationships, she's unable to conform to societal expectations and has displayed a consistent inability to form genuine connections.

These criteria, heavily impactful and persistently occurring since youth, might lead to a genuine diagnosis of ASPD. A true ASPD diagnosis requires a persistent, inflexible pattern of severe behavioral issues that interfere with multiple aspects of life, starting in early adolescence and continuing into adulthood.

Gender and Antisocial Personality Disorder

The DSM-V reports that ASPD is significantly more common in men than in women, with diagnosis rates showing a pronounced gender gap. Studies also suggest that men are diagnosed with ASPD at a rate three to five times higher than women (Alegria et al., 2013).

While the underlying reasons for this discrepancy are complex, they may be influenced by both biological and sociocultural factors. Some research indicates that testosterone levels, brain structure differences, and genetic predispositions may contribute to the higher prevalence of ASPD in men.

Additionally, societal expectations and gender norms may shape how antisocial behaviors manifest and are perceived. For instance, men with ASPD often exhibit overt aggression and criminality, behaviors that align with traditional male stereotypes, making them more likely to be recognized and diagnosed.

In contrast, women with antisocial traits may express them in less overtly aggressive ways, which often leads to underdiagnosis or misdiagnosis. Rather than engaging in physical violence or openly defying authority, women with ASPD may exhibit more relational aggression, manipulativeness, or subtle deception.

The DSM-V acknowledges that women who display antisocial behaviors are more likely to be diagnosed with other co-existing disorders, especially those that include heightened emotional dysregulation and fear of abandonment (American Psychiatric Association, 2013).

These distinctions can significantly shape how the disorder is recognized or overlooked. For men, ASPD symptoms might more frequently align with outwardly aggressive behaviors and criminal activity, which are much more likely to be noticed.

In contrast, women may sometimes exhibit manipulation in more relational contexts, utilizing deceit in ways that are less overtly aggressive but can be equally detrimental. For instance, women might manipulate through social climbing or by distorting relational dynamics, while men may do so through intimidation and more direct threats.

The Evolution of Antisocial Personality Disorder: A Historical Perspective

Perceptions of the behaviors and characteristics associated with antisocial personality disorder have shifted dramatically over time, mirroring broader changes in how society defines morality, criminality, and mental illness. In the 19th century, individuals exhibiting the same traits now associated with the disorder were often labeled instead as suffering from "moral insanity"—a term that suggested a defect in character rather than a diagnosable psychological condition (Ozarin, 2001).

This perspective, rooted in conservative Victorian-era notions of social order, framed such individuals as lacking the morality to adhere to social norms. As such, legal and medical institutions responded with punishment rather than rehabilitation, which failed to have any lasting impacts on either individuals or society.

Even early psychiatric studies on the condition failed to understand its nuance properly. Psychiatrist Hervey Cleckley's seminal work, *The Mask of Sanity* (1941), introduced a broad understanding of antisocial behavior under the larger umbrella of psychopathy, describing individuals who appeared superficially charming and intelligent yet lacked empathy and exhibited chronic deceitfulness. However, this work focused mostly on the darkest and most violent behaviors and provided a somewhat limited understanding of the frequency of antisocial personality disorder.

Fortunately, clinician Robert Hare built upon Cleckley's research with his development of the Psychopathy Checklist-Revised (PCL-R), a clinical tool that remains widely used in forensic psychology. This research would help support the refinement of the American Psychiatric Association's overall diagnostic criteria for a range of disorders (Salekin et al., 1996).

In fact, early editions of the *Diagnostic and Statistical Manual of Mental Disorders* (DSM) focused almost exclusively on outwardly antisocial actions, such as habitual lawbreaking. However, later versions—including the DSM-III and DSM-IV—began to incorporate a deeper understanding of personality dysfunction, emphasizing traits such as impulsivity, lack of remorse, and manipulativeness, as well as a range of other mental health challenges (Pickersgill, 2011).

The current DSM-V criteria reflect this evolution, recognizing ASPD as a pervasive and maladaptive pattern of disregard for the rights of others rather than a moral failing.

Shifting Response

Early responses to individuals with antisocial traits were overwhelmingly punitive. In the early 20th century, incarceration, institutionalization, and even forced sterilization were common methods of managing those deemed to have "psychopathic personalities" (Black, 2015).

The underlying assumption was that such individuals were inherently dangerous and incapable of change, and so fear of imprisonment or consequences was the only available recourse. However, as psychological research advanced, it became clear that punishment alone did little to address the root causes of antisocial behavior. In some cases, incarceration may have even reinforced manipulative and violent tendencies, as individuals with ASPD often adapt to exploitative environments in ways that exacerbate their harmful behaviors.

By the late 20th century, cognitive-behavioral therapy (CBT) emerged as a leading approach for treating ASPD, with some success in helping individuals recognize and modify destructive thought patterns. Although ASPD remains notoriously difficult to treat, especially in individuals with high levels of psychopathy, some interventions have shown promise, particularly those focusing on impulse control, emotional regulation, and the development of prosocial behaviors.

Beyond therapy, research has also explored neurobiological factors, including differences in brain structure and function, which could eventually open doors to new treatment approaches (Carr, 2024).

Cultural perspectives also shape how ASPD is understood and managed. In collectivist societies, where interpersonal harmony is highly valued, traits such as manipulation and deceitfulness may be less tolerated than in more individualistic cultures, where assertiveness and strategic self-interest are sometimes rewarded. This has led to debates about whether ASPD is universally defined or if its diagnosis is influenced by cultural biases (Mulder, 2012). Clinicians working with diverse populations must consider these nuances, ensuring that diagnoses reflect true psychological dysfunction rather than culturally specific behaviors.

The evolving understanding of ASPD reflects its complexity. While some individuals with the disorder can learn to manage their behavior, others remain a significant challenge for clinicians, legal systems, and society. In that sense, striking a balance between empathy and vigilance is necessary, recognizing the humanity of those with ASPD while accurately acknowledging and assessing the potential risks they pose.

The Larger Impact of Common Behaviors in Antisocial Personalities

Antisocial personality disorder is more than a collection of isolated negative behaviors—it is a deeply ingrained, persistent pattern of manipulation, deceit, and disregard for others. Individuals with ASPD do not merely struggle with understanding or acting on social norms; they often actively violate them, typically with a chilling absence of remorse.

While many people occasionally act selfishly or impulsively, those with ASPD exhibit these behaviors as defining traits of their personality. Taking a closer look at some of these behaviors can help us form a deeper understanding of the disorder, but can also aid in identifying individuals who may pose a danger to others as early as possible.

Chronic Deceit

A defining feature of ASPD is chronic deceit. Individuals with this disorder are often pathological liars, using dishonesty as a tool to manipulate, exploit, or control others. Unlike a person who lies to avoid embarrassment or conflict, someone with ASPD lies habitually—even when the truth would serve them just as well.

Their deception is not simply a means to an end but a fundamental aspect of their interactions with the world. This manipulativeness extends beyond lying; they often engage in elaborate schemes for financial, social, or even sadistic gain. For instance, they may con a friend into lending them money with no intention of repaying it or feign remorse after being caught in an act of infidelity, only to repeat the behavior without hesitation.

In particular, those with the disorder often possess a chameleon-like quality in their interactions, morphing to fit their surroundings and needs. Picture someone who changes their story fluidly depending on the audience, weaving deceit with alarming skill. In personal relationships, this might manifest as crafting elaborate lies to avoid accountability or gain an advantage over others.

Lack of Empathy and Disregard For Others

Perhaps the most dangerous hallmark of ASPD is a lack of empathy. While most people experience guilt or remorse after harming others, individuals with ASPD are typically indifferent to the suffering they cause.

While they may *appear* remorseful under pressure, they don't experience regret in the way a normal person would; instead, they typically only show remorse when consequences negatively impact them and often respond by justifying or dismissing their harmful actions. This can be seen in everything from financial fraud to violent crime—behaviors carried out without a second thought for the victims involved. This callousness allows them to exploit others with ease, whether by manipulating a loved one into financial ruin or coercing someone into dangerous or illegal activities.

Aggressiveness is a related trait, though it's important to understand that it may not always manifest in overt violence. Some individuals with ASPD react with explosive rage at minor inconveniences, lashing out physically or verbally, while others express their hostility through cold, calculated psychological manipulation and attempts to control and overpower others. This aggression can manifest in relationships where they use intimidation, threats, or outright violence to control their partners or family members.

Impulsivity and Reckless Decision-Making

Impulsivity is a defining trait of ASPD, driving individuals to act without considering the long-term consequences. Impulsivity and excess risk-taking naturally extend from the detachment and manipulation discussed earlier.

People with ASPD frequently act without considering the consequences, driven by a desire for immediate gratification. Consider someone racing through traffic, indifferent to the danger posed to themselves and others, or making spur-of-the-moment financial decisions without regard for future repercussions.

Unlike someone who makes an occasional reckless decision, a person with ASPD consistently prioritizes immediate gratification over long-term stability. This can make them especially dangerous in positions of power, as they may make rash business decisions, betray professional colleagues, or endanger others without a moment's hesitation. This impulsivity also contributes to criminal activity. While not all individuals with ASPD are violent offenders, many have a history of arrests, fraud, theft, or other legal violations.

Disregard For Rules

Additionally, a disregard for social norms commonly appears in individuals with ASPD. They often flaunt societal rules, perhaps viewing them as restrictive or irrelevant. Envision someone consistently flouting workplace regulations or engaging in minor criminal acts with little concern for societal judgment or legal repercussions.

Understanding this tendency allows for more informed interactions, enabling people to navigate social or professional environments with increased awareness and caution. While not all who feel resistance to rules or structure have ASPD, rule-breaking behaviors can be a red flag to increase one's vigilance and take notice of other behaviors for signs of an antisocial personality.

The Power of Recognizing Antisocial Behavioral Patterns

Understanding the behaviors associated with ASPD can be incredibly valuable, not just for mental health professionals but for everyone. While individual traits such as impulsivity or deceitfulness do not necessarily indicate ASPD, when these behaviors form a persistent and overarching pattern, they become a cause for concern and likely indicate individuals against whom you want to defend yourself.

Recognizing the warning signs early can help individuals protect themselves from emotional, financial, and even physical harm. It can also help you safeguard yourself against criminal behavior, as those with ASPD are far more likely to commit crimes; in fact, the prevalence of ASPD among incarcerated individuals ranges from 46% to 84% (Seid et al., 2022), which is far higher than the 1-4% found in the general population.

Case Study: The Quiet Neighbor

John Mitchell, a 42-year-old man, was well-known in his suburban neighborhood as a quiet, unassuming individual. He lived alone in a modest, well-kept house on the corner of a leafy street. Neighbors would describe him as friendly but somewhat reserved, someone who kept to himself but was always willing to help out when asked. He had a steady job as an accountant at a mid-sized firm and, despite his private nature, seemed like any other average middle-class man.

As neighbors began exchanging observations, several behaviors emerged that altered the perception of this quiet presence. For instance, sudden antagonistic actions without obvious provocation occurred, often in disputes over property lines or noise levels.

Such conflicts provided a window into a more aggressive and impulsive persona than initially expected. Additionally, this person showed an uncanny ability to charm new arrivals with a pleasant demeanor before subtly alienating them from others, thus creating fractured community ties.

Early Warning Signs

John's issues with authority began at a young age. Growing up in a lower-income neighborhood, he was often in trouble with school officials and local law enforcement for petty theft, vandalism, and physical altercations with peers. His parents, unable to handle his increasingly disruptive behavior, sought therapy, but John quickly learned how to manipulate adults and present himself as the misunderstood victim. By the age of 16, he was caught stealing from a local store but was let off with a warning. This marked the beginning of his long history of criminal behavior.

Throughout his teenage years, John frequently lied to his friends, family, and teachers. He was a master of deception, often telling elaborate stories to make himself seem more impressive than he truly was. For example, he claimed to be a star athlete, even though he had never played any competitive sport. His ability to charm and deceive people made it difficult for others to see through his façade, and even those closest to him were often unaware of the extent of his manipulations.

John's Double Life

As an adult, John continued to engage in criminal activities, but he became much more calculated and discreet in his approach. He moved into his current neighborhood under the guise of a hardworking accountant who preferred to live a simple, quiet life. His neighbors admired him for his punctuality and his willingness to lend a helping hand when needed. He often volunteered for neighborhood watch duties, and no one suspected that the man who spoke so kindly about community safety was, in fact, a threat to it.

Behind closed doors, however, John's life was far more sinister. He was involved in a series of financial scams, including embezzling money from his workplace and using stolen identities to open credit accounts. He had no remorse for these actions; in fact, he viewed them as nothing more than a game—one that he was winning.

His manipulations were not limited to finances, however. He routinely lied to his family, convincing them that he had been promoted at work or was attending prestigious events, even though he had no such achievements.

John's relationships were also marked by emotional abuse and manipulation. His romantic partners often reported that he could be charming and affectionate one moment and cold and distant the next. When his partners began to question his behavior or confront him about his lies, he would quickly turn the tables, making them feel guilty for doubting him.

On several occasions, when his partners threatened to leave him, John resorted to intimidation and threats of violence. In one instance, he told an ex-girlfriend that if she ever reported him to the police, he would make sure she lost custody of her children. His threats were not idle; John had a history of using physical violence to control others. In fact, he had been arrested twice for assault in the past, though each time he was able to manipulate his way out of serious legal consequences.

Aggression and Control

John's violent tendencies were not confined to his relationships. He had been involved in several physical altercations, including a violent road rage incident where he rammed another driver's car off the road. He later justified his actions by claiming that the other driver had been "asking for it" by cutting him off. His lack of empathy and complete disregard for the safety and well-being of others were evident in every aspect of his life.

What made John particularly dangerous was his ability to control the narrative around him. When people became suspicious of his behavior, he would quickly charm his way back into their good graces, often playing the role of the misunderstood underdog. He would offer excuses for his actions, often blaming others or claiming that circumstances had forced him to make difficult decisions. This manipulation allowed him to maintain a façade of normalcy while continuing his harmful behaviors in secret.

John's double life began to unravel when a neighbor, Sarah, grew suspicious of his increasingly erratic behavior. She had noticed that he seemed to be spending more time at home, and he was acting strangely toward other neighbors. His once cordial demeanor had turned cold and dismissive, and he had become more confrontational during neighborhood meetings. When Sarah became concerned about the financial schemes she suspected John was involved in, she decided to confront him.

A tense conversation followed in which John denied everything, turning the situation around to make Sarah feel guilty for questioning him. However, Sarah had done her research, and after some investigation, she was able to uncover a trail of fraudulent financial transactions and violent incidents. Armed with this evidence, she went to the police, leading to John's eventual arrest.

In court, it was revealed that John had been living a life full of deceit, manipulation, and violence. His diagnosis of ASPD was confirmed, and it became clear that his charming exterior hid a deeply disturbed and dangerous individual.

John's case serves as a stark reminder that those with ASPD can lead double lives, appearing to be perfectly ordinary on the surface while engaging in behaviors that are harmful, manipulative, and even criminal.

From a psychological perspective, such cases are significant illustrations of the importance of knowledge and vigilance. Recognizing problematic traits early can provide clues that allow you to remove yourself from harm's way. This neighbor's lack of long-term planning, evident in sporadic employment and abrupt lifestyle changes, signified core ASPD issues of irresponsibility and impulsivity.

Observing how disregard for societal norms plays out in seemingly inconsequential behaviors, like repeated driving infractions or non-payment of community dues, provides insight into a broader picture of personality dysfunction and can be a signal to take extra caution that protects you or your community.

Beneath the Surface

As you begin to learn to pick up on clues of potential danger, the patterns of ASPD are foundational to understanding and to begin to empower ourselves to navigate social environments with greater awareness and caution.

Identifying manipulative, impulsive, and norm-violating behaviors equips us to see beyond façades, helping us understand when an individual's seemingly quiet and unassuming exterior masks deeper volatility and a harmful personality. This knowledge not only allows us to proactively address potential risks but also to ensure safer communities.

The core behaviors linked to ASPD—characterized by deceit, impulsivity, and disregard for societal rules—can have profound effects, especially if not noticed early on. Recognizing these signs is of great value not only for personal safety but also for professionals like law enforcement, teachers, and social workers, all of whom can use it to prevent victimization.

In the next chapter, we'll move beyond the behavior and traits and take a closer look at the dark inner workings of the mind of a sociopath.

Chapter 2:

Chaotic and Calculated—Inside the Mind of the Sociopath

The term "sociopath" often conjures images of unpredictable individuals driven by volatile emotions and erratic behavior. However, beneath the apparent chaos lies a deeper, more calculated set of mechanisms that govern their actions.

Imagine sitting across from an acquaintance, catching up over coffee. They recount tales of childhood mischief, sprinkle in a few compliments, and appear so relatable that you feel instantly at ease. Yet, beneath their genial façade lies a mind adept at reading people, exploiting vulnerabilities, and crafting narratives to suit their own agenda. You might find yourself questioning if every interaction was genuine or simply part of a calculated plan. This unpredictable blend of charm and cunning is not uncommon, yet it creates an unsettling uncertainty for those caught in its sway.

Sociopaths, another term for individuals diagnosed with antisocial personality disorder (ASPD), as discussed in the previous chapter, exhibit a profound disconnect from societal norms and a pervasive disregard for others' rights. Yet, despite their outward disorderliness, many demonstrate remarkable precision in their manipulations, forming strategies that benefit their personal agendas.

In this chapter, we'll explore the labyrinthine of sociopathy, the nature versus nurture debate, and what shapes the inner workings of those with ASPD. We'll examine how genetic predispositions and environmental influences intertwine to shape the chaotic yet calculating mental structure of sociopathic behavior and the internal motivations and workings that drive it.

Through this lens, we'll also aim to understand the overall psychology of sociopaths better, in a way that can help you prevent becoming a victim of their methodical manipulation and remorseless harm.

Nature vs. Nurture Debate in Sociopathy

The behavioral manifestations of sociopathy are widely recognized, which we covered earlier, and are so common that they've been classified as a pathology known in psychiatry as ASPD. On the other hand, the inner workings and causes of sociopathy continue to intrigue both scientists and psychologists.

While there is a range of theories about the root causes for the patterns and behaviors of sociopathy, its origins are far from clear. In fact, the debate over whether sociopathy arises from genetic predispositions (nature) or environmental factors (nurture) has been a focal point of psychological and sociological research for decades. On one hand, genetic and biological theories suggest that sociopathy may have a neurological or hereditary basis.

Research has shown that individuals with sociopathic traits often display irregularities in brain functioning, particularly in areas responsible for impulse control, empathy, and moral reasoning, such as the prefrontal cortex. Some studies suggest that there may be a genetic predisposition to these behaviors, with a family history of personality disorders or criminal activity increasing the likelihood of sociopathic tendencies (Tuvblad & Beaver, 2013). This line of thinking posits that sociopaths may be "born that way," with an inherent neurological disposition toward antisocial behavior.

While genetics may play a role, we can't dismiss the environment's role in shaping sociopathic tendencies. Childhood trauma, neglect, or abuse are common in the histories of many individuals diagnosed with sociopathy. These early life experiences can disrupt the development of empathy, social bonds, and a sense of moral responsibility.

Research shows that sociopaths often come from dysfunctional family backgrounds or environments where violence, manipulation, and deceit were modeled as acceptable behaviors (Bonn, 2014). Thus, proponents of the nurture theory argue that sociopathy can result not merely from an innate or biological predisposition but from the negative influences of a harmful upbringing, where individuals learn maladaptive coping mechanisms and dysfunctional relationship patterns (Kaufman, 2010).

In reality, sociopathy is likely to be caused by a combination of both nature and nurture, with genetic predispositions interacting with environmental factors to influence the development of ASPD. Some individuals may have a genetic vulnerability that, under the right circumstances, manifests in antisocial behaviors. Others, lacking such a genetic predisposition, may still develop sociopathic traits due to exposure to severe trauma or neglect.

Perhaps most significantly, as we continue to explore the mind of the sociopath and the origins of their harmful behaviors, it becomes increasingly clear that this is not a matter of inherent evil or moral failure. Understanding the roots of sociopathy, whether biological, environmental, or a combination of both, can help us understand the nuances that allow us to identify early warning signs for personal protection and reduce the broader societal impact of sociopathic behaviors through intervention.

Sociopathy vs. Psychopathy

Sociopathy and psychopathy are two terms often used interchangeably to describe individuals with antisocial traits or behaviors, but they are, in fact, distinct concepts with significant differences in their origins, behaviors, and emotional profiles. Both sociopathy and psychopathy fall under the umbrella of ASPD.

Despite the overlap in some behavioral symptoms, sociopathy and psychopathy differ in their emotional functioning, relationship styles, impulsivity, and the underlying causes of their traits. This distinction is important as it shapes how individuals with these conditions interact with others, their potential for change, and the way they are treated in clinical and forensic settings.

Emotional Responses and Empathy

One of the primary distinctions between sociopathy and psychopathy lies in the emotional responses of individuals with these conditions. While both sociopaths and psychopaths lack empathy, the nature of their emotional detachment varies.

Sociopathy

Sociopaths can experience some form of emotion, particularly anger or frustration, which often drives their impulsive and reactive behavior. They may also form limited attachments to certain individuals, although these connections are often self-serving and dysfunctional.

Sociopaths are more likely to act based on emotional triggers, which can lead to erratic and unpredictable behavior. Their emotional responses are often intense and unstable, and their actions may be driven by feelings of anger, betrayal, or a desire for revenge.

Despite these emotional impulses, sociopaths are still largely indifferent to the feelings of others.

Psychopathy

Psychopaths, on the other hand, tend to be emotionally shallow and often lack any true emotional connection to others. They do not experience the full range of emotions that most people do. Instead of anger or frustration, they may experience more calculated feelings of entitlement or superiority.

Psychopaths can mimic emotions and may even be adept at feigning care or concern when it benefits them, but these emotions are typically superficial and manipulative.

Psychopaths do not form genuine emotional bonds, and their lack of empathy is profound, extending beyond personal relationships to the broader societal implications of their actions. Unlike sociopaths, psychopaths do not experience strong emotional reactions to situations; their behavior is colder and more calculated, driven by an intellectual assessment of what will benefit them.

Impulsivity and Decision-Making

Another key difference between sociopathy and psychopathy is how the two types of individuals approach decision-making, particularly in high-stakes or risky situations. This distinction is largely tied to the impulsivity of sociopaths versus the planned, deliberate nature of psychopaths.

Sociopathy

Sociopaths tend to be more impulsive and reactive in their behavior. They may act without considering the long-term consequences of their actions, driven by immediate desires or emotional responses. For example, a sociopath may engage in violent behavior, substance abuse, or criminal activity as a direct response to frustration, anger, or stress. This impulsivity can lead to chaotic, erratic behavior that is often unpredictable and not carefully thought out.

Sociopaths may act on whim or instinct, responding to environmental cues or internal emotional states rather than planning their actions in advance. This impulsive nature often makes their behavior more volatile and difficult to predict, and they are more likely to engage in risky or criminal actions on the spur of the moment.

Psychopathy

Psychopaths, in contrast, are more calculated and deliberate in their actions. They are less likely to act impulsively, and when they do engage in harmful or criminal behavior, it is typically well-planned and thought out. Psychopaths excel in manipulating others and often take a long-term approach to achieving their goals, carefully considering the risks and benefits of their actions.

They are able to control their impulses and delay gratification in order to secure a greater personal advantage. This calculated nature makes psychopaths highly dangerous, as they can act in ways that are not immediately obvious, and their planning can extend to creating elaborate schemes or deceptions to achieve their objectives.

Psychopaths tend to view people as tools or objects to be used for their personal gain, and they are patient in their pursuit of these goals, often spending considerable time and energy to manipulate their environment.

Relationships and Attachment

Both sociopaths and psychopaths struggle with forming meaningful social bonds, but their relationship styles differ considerably in terms of emotional investment, attachment, and even styles of manipulation.

Sociopathy

Sociopaths are often capable of forming attachments, although these connections are typically self-serving. They may form strong attachments to a small group of individuals—such as a close friend, family member, or romantic partner—but these relationships tend to be marked by manipulation and control.

Sociopaths may view others as tools for their own benefit, but they can experience a limited form of loyalty or affection toward certain people. However, their emotional connections are often unstable, and they can easily betray or abandon those they claim to care about.

Sociopaths tend to be volatile in their relationships, as their behaviors are often driven by frustration, anger, or the desire to assert control.

Psychopathy

Psychopaths, in contrast, are incapable of forming genuine emotional attachments. They may be charming or charismatic, capable of winning the trust of others, but their relationships are primarily manipulative and exploitative.

Psychopaths use their superficial charm and social skills to deceive others and achieve their personal goals, but these interactions are typically devoid of genuine emotional investment. They may create relationships that appear normal on the surface, but these connections are often based on lies, manipulation, and control.

Psychopaths do not care for others in the way that most people do; rather, they view relationships as opportunities to extract resources or power from others. They may feign affection, empathy, or concern, but these emotions are hollow and calculated, designed to maintain control or gain an advantage.

Risk to Society and Criminal Behavior

Both sociopaths and psychopaths pose significant risks to society, but their methods and levels of danger differ.

Sociopathy

Sociopaths tend to act impulsively and are more likely to be caught in the act of committing crimes or engaging in violent behavior. Their impulsivity and emotional reactivity often lead to confrontations with others, and they are more likely to be aggressive or violent in response to perceived slights or frustrations.

Sociopaths are also more likely to engage in criminal behavior out of immediate needs, such as financial gain, revenge, or the desire to control others.

Psychopaths, on the other hand, are often more calculating and less likely to be detected for their criminal behavior. Their ability to plan and manipulate others makes them particularly dangerous, as they are less likely to be caught or punished for their actions.

Psychopaths can engage in long-term criminal activities, such as fraud, embezzlement, or organized crime, and they are often able to maintain a façade of normalcy, blending in with society while secretly engaging in harmful behaviors.

Because of their emotional detachment and calculating nature, psychopaths can operate in more covert and sophisticated ways, making them harder to identify and stop.

Psychological Traits of Sociopaths: Potential Causes and Influences

Sociopathy fascinates and terrifies, a testament to its complexity within human behavior. Now that we've explored the nature versus nurture debate, acknowledging that sociopathy often emerges from a tangled blend of genetic predisposition and environmental influence, we can begin to peel back layers of what makes a sociopath tick, starting with their defining psychological traits.

Each of these traits—lack of empathy, manipulative tendencies, impulsivity, irresponsibility, narcissism, and deceit—can be traced back to a combination of biological factors and environmental conditions.

Lack of Empathy: Neurological Deficits and Early Trauma

A fundamental characteristic of sociopathy is an absence of empathy, a stark divergence from typical human behavior. Empathy typically allows us to connect with others, but in sociopaths, it's often glaringly absent. They can't easily relate to the emotions and experiences of others, which also limits their ability to form genuine bonds and relationships.

This lack of emotional connectivity potentially has strong biological underpinnings. Studies using brain imaging have found that sociopaths often have an underactive amygdala—the part of the brain responsible for processing emotions, particularly fear and empathy (Yang et al., 2009).

This neurological deficit makes it difficult for them to experience both a sympathetic experience of the feelings of others, as well as guilt or remorse, even in situations where others would be overwhelmed with emotion. For example, research has shown that when sociopaths are shown images that typically evoke distress, such as a crying child or a grieving parent, they display significantly less brain activation compared to typical individuals (Plackett, 2021).

On the environmental side, early childhood trauma or neglect can also play a significant role. Children who experience extreme emotional deprivation, abuse, or chaotic family dynamics often fail to develop healthy emotional responses (McLean, 2018). For example, if a child learns early on that expressing emotions leads to punishment or that vulnerability invites harm, they may unconsciously suppress empathy as a survival mechanism and eventually have an underdeveloped ability to emotionally connect as part of their core personality.

Manipulative Nature: Genetic Predisposition and Modeled Behavior

Sociopaths typically view relationships not as mutual exchanges but as opportunities for personal gain. Their relational distortion may not be immediately apparent but often becomes evident as they exploit situations to further their own ends, indifferent to the emotional toll on others. This behavior can manifest in subtle ways, such as charming their way into a promotion, or in more extreme forms, like orchestrating elaborate frauds or deception for personal benefit.

Some research suggests that manipulative tendencies may have a genetic basis. Certain personality traits, such as Machiavellianism and a predisposition for deceit, have been linked to heritable factors (Jones & Paulhus, 2017). Twin studies indicate that antisocial behavior has a moderate to high degree of heritability, meaning that children of sociopathic individuals are more likely to develop similar traits (Segal, 1995).

However, manipulation is also often a learned behavior, both due to normalization in their environment or as a means to survive. A child raised in an environment where deceit and exploitation are normalized—whether through criminal parents, abusive caregivers, or exposure to toxic social dynamics—may adopt these behaviors. Additionally, if a child had needs that weren't naturally met, they may have adapted manipulation of others as a survival strategy, internalizing it as a standard approach to relationships (Liubov, 2013).

Superficial Charm: Neurological Rewards and Social Conditioning

Many sociopaths can be incredibly charismatic. In fact, they often wear likeability as a disguise for their darker intentions. Imagine someone who dazzles at parties with charm and wit but is calculating the best way to use these newfound connections for selfish purposes. This charm complicates the early detection of sociopathy. It's typically much later, perhaps when their interests clash with yours, that the charm reveals itself as a façade.

From a biological standpoint, sociopaths often exhibit heightened activity in the brain's reward system, particularly in dopamine pathways. Dopamine, a neurotransmitter associated with pleasure and reward, plays a large role in how individuals perceive and respond to social cues. Sociopaths may have an enhanced sensitivity to rewards, which influences their socialization strategies (Buckholtz et al., 2010). Their charm may also stem from an innate ability to read social cues and respond in a way that maximizes personal gain. This ability to mimic emotional responses—without genuinely feeling them—may allow them to navigate social situations with ease.

Social conditioning also plays a role. If a child learns early on that charm can be used to manipulate others into desired behavior and avoid punishment or other consequences, they may have refined this skill over time. Sociopaths who receive reinforcement—whether through financial gain, admiration, or power—may have learned that their charm is a valuable tool for exploitation and honed it accordingly.

Impulsivity: Frontal Lobe Dysfunction and Unstable Upbringing

Sociopaths often exhibit rashness, making decisions in pursuit of short-term thrills rather than considering long-term consequences. This impulsivity can splinter relationships and damage careers, leaving chaos in the wake of recklessness and foolish behaviors.

One of the strongest biological contributors to impulsivity is dysfunction in the prefrontal cortex—the area of the brain responsible for decision-making and self-control. Studies have shown that sociopaths tend to have lower activity in this region, which impairs their ability to regulate impulsive urges (Koenigs, 2012). This neurological deficiency means they struggle with delayed gratification and are more prone to reckless behavior.

In terms of environmental influence, an unstable upbringing can exacerbate impulsive tendencies. Children who grow up in chaotic households—where rules are inconsistent or constantly changing—may never develop the ability to think ahead or consider consequences. If they see impulsive behavior rewarded, or at least not punished, they are more likely to carry that pattern into adulthood (Bezdjian et al., 2011).

Narcissistic Tendencies: Genetic Influence and Reinforced Entitlement

Sociopaths often carry an inflated sense of self-importance. They see themselves as superior, dismissing others' thoughts and feelings as secondary or irrelevant. This narcissism can be particularly destructive, as it makes it easier for sociopaths to perceive their actions and values through a lens of self-interest.

There is evidence that narcissistic tendencies have a genetic component. Research indicates that individuals with sociopathic traits often have parents or relatives with similar personality structures (Segal, 1995). Additionally, neurobiological factors—such as an overactive dopamine system—may contribute to an inflated sense of self-worth, as sociopaths seek constant stimulation and rewards.

Entitlement can also be reinforced through environmental factors. A child raised in a setting where they are constantly told they are superior, where they get away with manipulative behavior, or where harmful behavior is never challenged, may develop an exaggerated sense of self-importance. Sociopaths who experience early success in deception or exploitation may further reinforce their belief that they are above societal norms.

Behavioral Patterns of Sociopaths

Having explored the foundational psychological traits of sociopathy in the previous section, we now shift our focus to the everyday behaviors sociopaths exhibit—examining not only how these behaviors manifest but also the underlying thought processes that drive them.

Sociopaths' lack of empathy, impulsivity, and superficial charm lay the groundwork for patterns of dishonesty, deceitfulness, aggression, hostility, social isolation, and exploitation. Each of these behaviors stems from a unique internal logic—one shaped by neurological differences, childhood experiences, and a distorted perception of relationships and morality. By understanding the internal landscape of sociopathy, we gain deeper insight into why sociopaths act as they do.

Dishonesty: A Strategic Tool

Dishonesty is a defining characteristic of sociopaths, revealing itself through habitual lying, half-truths, and deception. Unlike neurotypical individuals who may experience guilt or cognitive dissonance when lying, sociopaths often view dishonesty as a strategic tool—something to be used whenever it serves their interests. They often don't distinguish between truth and falsehood in an ethical sense but instead consider which option is most advantageous in a given moment (Silvers, 2024).

Their thought process revolves around a simple calculation—whether the lie will benefit them, whether they can manipulate their way out if caught, and whether controlling someone's perception gives them power.

Additionally, because they do not experience the same anxiety or moral hesitation that usually accompanies deception, their lies are often delivered with confidence and are more believable. If exposed, they rarely admit fault, instead layering new lies to maintain control of the narrative.

Neurologically, reduced connectivity between the prefrontal cortex, the part of the brain that governs impulse control, and the amygdala, which processes fear and moral emotions, plays a role in this behavior (Plackett, 2021).

In many cases, childhood environments that normalized deception—whether through necessity or by example—further reinforce it and often contribute to the ability to lie or deceive effortlessly.

Aggression and Hostility

Aggression, another common sociopathic trait, stems from impulsivity and a need for dominance. While psychopaths often use calculated aggression to achieve long-term goals, sociopaths tend to be explosively reactive, easily provoked by perceived slights or obstacles.

Their inability to regulate emotions means they lash out when frustrated, often escalating minor conflicts into full-blown confrontations. Beneath the surface, their thought process is simple: if they do not immediately assert control, they risk appearing weak.

Closely linked to aggression is hostility, which manifests as chronic resentment, sarcasm, or outright cruelty. Unlike impulsive aggression, hostility is more calculated—a simmering belief that the world is against them and that people are either obstacles or enemies. They assume others are as self-serving and deceitful as they are, which creates deep-seated suspicion.

A sociopath's internal monologue is often colored by paranoia, an expectation of betrayal, and a conviction that kindness is either manipulative or weak. This results in a pattern of condescension, mockery, and emotional outbursts designed to belittle others and reinforce their own sense of superiority.

Over time, the aggression and hostility of a sociopath alienate those around them, yet they rarely see themselves as the cause. Instead, they frame their isolation as proof that most people are incompetent, foolish, or incapable of handling the "truth." In many cases, this perspective stems from early experiences of neglect or betrayal, which condition them to see relationships as inherently problematic and difficult.

Exploitation

Building on their manipulative tendencies and superficial charm, sociopaths often escalate to outright exploitation. Whether through emotional manipulation, financial scams, or coercive tactics, sociopaths see others as tools to be used rather than as individuals with their own agency. Their internal monologue is often predatory—focused on identifying vulnerabilities and extracting as much value as possible before moving on. They do not experience guilt over their actions because they do not see others as fully human in the way neurotypical individuals do.

Their ability to exploit stems from a combination of charm, deception, and intimidation. When one tactic fails, they seamlessly pivot to another, always seeking the most effective way to achieve their goal. Studies suggest that sociopaths have an overactive striatum, the brain structure that makes one more likely to prioritize immediate gratification over long-term consequences (Plackett, 2021). If their early environment rewarded cunning and manipulation, they may have internalized the belief that power belongs to those willing to take it—by any means necessary.

Rather than feeling remorse or guilt, a sociopath will typically move on from exploiting someone when that person is no longer useful to them—whether because they've extracted all they can, the person has become too difficult to manipulate, or a more appealing target has appeared.

Since sociopaths operate with a cost-benefit mindset, they don't waste time on situations that no longer serve them. Their decision to disengage is rarely emotional or morally driven; it's purely strategic.

Case Study: The Charismatic Conman

James Delaney had an uncanny ability to make people feel like they were the most important person in the room. He wasn't just confident—he radiated certainty. His handshake was firm, his tailored suit impeccable, and his easygoing smile instantly put others at ease.

To those who met him, he wasn't just another businessman; he was a financial genius with a golden touch. James spoke the language of success fluently, peppering conversations with just enough jargon to sound credible but not so much as to be intimidating.

The Con

His scam always began the same way—positioning himself as an insider with exclusive knowledge of an emerging investment opportunity. He never approached just anyone; he targeted those who were financially stable but still hungry for more—entrepreneurs, retirees looking to grow their nest eggs, and ambitious professionals eager to break into high-stakes investing. He presented himself as a mentor, someone who had already "made it" and was willing to take others under his wing.

What set James apart was his ability to build the trust of others quickly. He had an innate instinct for identifying what people wanted to hear—whether it was financial freedom, an escape from corporate drudgery, or a legacy to leave behind. He made his victims feel like they had been carefully selected, subtly flattering them into believing they were part of an elite circle. The more he emphasized exclusivity, the more eager they became to be included.

Sociopaths don't just rely on logic to persuade; they use emotion. James knew that fear and greed were the two greatest motivators in financial decision-making, and he used both to his advantage. He painted a picture of a once-in-a-lifetime opportunity, subtly implying that only the truly smart investors would recognize its value before it took off.

But the real genius of his manipulation lay in the way he neutralized doubt. If a potential investor hesitated, he wouldn't argue—instead, he'd feign indifference. *"Look," he'd say with a knowing smile, "I totally get it. Some people just aren't comfortable taking risks, and that's fine. I've got a dozen others lined up who'd kill for this chance."* By making it seem like the opportunity was slipping away, he triggered urgency and the fear of missing out, pushing people to invest before they had time to think critically.

If someone expressed skepticism, he would subtly undermine their confidence. *"I get that you're being cautious," he'd say, "but that's how most people miss out. The real players? They see past their fear and take action."* This played on his targets' egos—no one wanted to be the fool who hesitated while others struck gold.

Once someone had invested, James reinforced their commitment through gaslighting. If returns didn't appear as promised, he wouldn't admit fault. Instead, he'd suggest that the investor had misunderstood, wasn't patient enough, or simply wasn't seeing the bigger picture. *"You need to trust the process," he'd insist. "This isn't some get-rich-quick scheme—it's long-term wealth creation."* Any concerns were met with smooth reassurances, making the victim feel unreasonable for doubting him.

James's Exit Strategy

Sociopaths have no emotional attachment to their victims, only to the benefits they provide. The moment a financial scam becomes too risky—when investors start asking too many questions, when legal scrutiny arises, or when fresh targets become harder to find—James would disappear. Sometimes, he'd make a dramatic exit, leaving investors in the lurch with a fabricated excuse: an emergency overseas, a sudden business failure, or even a health crisis. Other times, he'd simply fade away, cutting off communication, leaving a trail of unanswered emails and unreturned calls.

By the time the scam unraveled, James was already setting up his next con in another city under a new name. For him, there were always more targets, more opportunities. The guilt, the devastation of his victims, the broken trust—none of it mattered.

Useful Insights

What makes sociopathic scammers so dangerous is their ability to manipulate human psychology with precision. Their success doesn't come from brute force or threats; it comes from making people *want* to trust them. Recognizing their tactics—love-bombing with flattery, creating artificial scarcity, exploiting emotions like greed and fear, gaslighting doubts—can serve as a defense against such schemes.

The best way to deter a sociopathic con artist is to deny them the reaction they seek. James thrived on persuasion and emotional influence. A potential victim who asked too many critical questions, insisted on independent verification, or refused to be rushed into a decision became a waste of time.

Sociopaths prefer easy marks; by demonstrating skepticism, a person increases the chances that the scammer will move on to a more gullible target. Understanding this mindset is the first step in preventing such manipulation and safeguarding against those who exploit trust for personal gain.

The Big Picture

To understand the inner workings of a sociopath is to step into a world where manipulation is second nature, emotions are tools, and human connection is a means to an end. We have taken a closer look at the origins and inner workings of sociopaths, including the interplay between genetic predispositions and environmental influences that shape these behaviors.

By recognizing the internal workings that underlie the manipulation, impulsivity, and lack of empathy that characterize sociopaths, you're far more able to equip yourself with strategies for protection, whether in personal interactions or professional engagements.

In the following chapter, we'll take a closer look at the complex inner world of the psychopath, a far more dangerous character to defend oneself against

Chapter 3:

Understanding Psychopathy—Charming Danger

Charming and elusive, Sam always seemed to be the life of the party. His charisma drew people in effortlessly. Those who met him only saw the smiles and heard the laughter, never suspecting a hidden agenda. Yet, beneath the surface of light-hearted conversations and friendly overtures was an emotional detachment that left others feeling strangely unsettled after the fact and might have provided clues into the undercurrents of manipulation that wove into his interactions.

In reality, his knack for reading people, alongside a lack of genuine empathy, allowed him to exploit vulnerabilities without any second thoughts. Due to a lack of remorse and a dangerous tendency to severely exploit others, Sam qualified as what we refer to as a psychopath.

The psychopath moves through the world observing, imitating, and manipulating others with mechanical precision while experiencing nearly no genuine human connection. Their charm is practiced, their empathy an illusion, their emotions a script they learn to play.

Unlike the sociopath, whose impulsive nature often betrays their lack of control, the psychopath is calculated and deliberate, which can make them far more dangerous. But what does it feel like to be inside the mind of a psychopath? What drives a person who lacks true emotional depth yet excels at mimicking it? How do they perceive morality, relationships, and the world itself?

This chapter will peel back the layers of the thought process of psychopaths, revealing a mental landscape where manipulation is second nature, control is paramount, and human connection is little more than a means to an end.

While to understand a psychopath is to understand a mind that operates on an entirely different frequency—one where emotions are tools, people are pieces on a chessboard, and life itself is a game to be won—this understanding can also be a source of safety.

Through recognizing subtle red flags of psychopathy, we become more equipped to identify these individuals and protect ourselves from their potential threat.

Are Psychopaths More Harmful Than Sociopaths? The Danger Debate

At first glance, psychopaths and sociopaths, both falling under the broader psychological diagnosis of antisocial personality disorder, may seem interchangeable. Both exhibit a lack of empathy, disregard societal norms, and manipulate others for personal gain. However, beneath the surface, their psychological distinctions are significant, shaping how they interact with the world and, more importantly, the level of potential threat they pose.

While sociopaths tend to be erratic, impulsive, and prone to emotional outbursts, psychopaths are cold, calculated, and methodically strategic. Understanding these distinctions—and the ongoing debate surrounding them—helps clarify why psychopaths are often considered the greater threat.

Clinical Distinctions and Controversies

The debate over the differences between psychopathy and sociopathy has persisted in psychological and criminological circles for decades. While neither term is officially recognized in the *Diagnostic and Statistical Manual of Mental Disorders* (DSM-V)—which instead uses antisocial personality disorder (ASPD) as a broad category—many experts argue that psychopathy and sociopathy represent distinct subtypes (DeAngelis, 2022).

Psychopathy is often associated with biological factors, particularly structural differences in the brain. Neuroimaging studies suggest that psychopaths exhibit reduced activity in the amygdala, which regulates fear and emotional processing, and the prefrontal cortex, which governs impulse control and decision-making (Plackett, 2021). This neurological wiring may explain their cold, calculated demeanor and lack of emotional depth. Psychopaths are believed to be born rather than made, their traits emerging early in life regardless of upbringing.

Sociopathy, by contrast, is more commonly linked to environmental factors, such as childhood trauma, abuse, or neglect. Unlike psychopaths, sociopaths do experience emotions, but their emotional regulation is poor, leading to impulsive, erratic, and sometimes violent behavior. Their antisocial tendencies are more reactive than premeditated, making them easier to identify and less effective in long-term manipulation.

Despite these distinctions, some psychologists argue that the psychopathy-sociopathy divide is overstated. They point to the spectrum-like nature of ASPD, where individuals exhibit varying degrees of emotional regulation, impulsivity, and manipulativeness (Haghighi, 2021).

Others criticize the focus on psychopathy as overly deterministic, cautioning that brain imaging alone cannot predict criminality or dangerousness with certainty (Aharoni et al., 2022). While these debates continue, most experts agree that psychopaths pose a greater long-term threat due to their ability to integrate seamlessly into society while engaging in harmful or even criminal behavior.

Impulse vs. Precision

One of the stark differences between sociopaths and psychopaths lies in impulse control. Sociopaths are typically far more prone to emotional outbursts, reckless decisions, and spur-of-the-moment aggression than psychopaths. Their behavior is often reactive, driven by anger, frustration, or perceived slights. Because of this, they frequently expose themselves, making it easier for others to recognize their manipulations or avoid them. A sociopath might lash out during an argument, sabotage a relationship in a fit of jealousy, or commit crimes without fully considering the long-term consequences.

Psychopaths, in contrast, are defined by their eerie self-control. They rarely act on impulse unless doing so serves a larger goal, such as to intimidate or distract someone. Their emotions—if they can even be called that—are shallow and detached, allowing them to calculate every move with cold precision. Unlike sociopaths, they meticulously plan ahead, mask their intentions, and execute their schemes without betraying their true nature.

Accordingly, psychopaths are more likely to manipulate their target over months or years, winning trust before exploiting them, whereas sociopaths are less likely to be able to do so without losing momentum or exposing their intentions.

When they commit crimes, psychopaths often do so methodically, covering their tracks to remain undetected. Their meticulous nature makes them far more insidious, as they can operate unnoticed for extended periods, even embedding themselves into positions of power and influence.

Social Integration: The Hidden Threat

Sociopaths may have initial charm or charisma but often struggle with long-term social integration. Their erratic behavior, inability to regulate emotions, and frequent conflicts often make it difficult for them to hold steady jobs or maintain long-term relationships.

Many sociopaths are drifters—individuals who engage in petty crime, struggle with addiction, or sabotage their own success due to poor impulse control. While this makes them dangerous on a personal level, their influence tends to be limited compared to psychopaths.

Psychopaths, on the other hand, are often experts at blending in and integrating socially. Highly intelligent psychopaths can achieve high-status positions—becoming CEOs, politicians, doctors, or even law enforcement officers. Their ability to mimic normal emotions allows them to gain trust and wield influence without raising suspicion. For example, whereas a sociopath might steal impulsively from their employer and get caught, a psychopath could infiltrate a corporation, orchestrate large-scale fraud, and walk away with millions without anyone suspecting foul play. This ability to manipulate entire systems—not just individuals—makes them not just potentially more threatening to individuals but a far greater societal threat (Silverio et al., 2023).

Emotional Detachment and the Capacity for Cruelty

Both sociopaths and psychopaths lack empathy, but the way this manifests is different. Sociopaths, while callous, can still form attachments, even if they are unhealthy or self-serving. They may develop an obsessive fixation on a partner, maintain loyalty to a close friend, or feel fleeting moments of guilt.

Psychopaths, on the other hand, are typically almost entirely emotionally hollow. They do not form genuine bonds, and any relationship they engage in is purely transactional. They can feign love, friendship, or concern, but it is all an act—a means to an end. This complete emotional detachment allows them to commit acts of cruelty without hesitation. Where a sociopath might lash out in a moment of rage, a psychopath can calmly torture, manipulate, or destroy someone without a second thought.

Their ability to harm others without remorse—while remaining composed and collected—is what makes them chillingly dangerous, as their harmful behaviors can be far more managed and, therefore, obscured.

Criminal Tendencies: Organized vs. Chaotic

Sociopaths often engage in reckless or violent criminal behavior. They commit crimes in fits of anger, make impulsive decisions that lead to their downfall, and rarely think ahead. Their crimes are disorganized, leaving behind evidence and drawing attention. Many end up incarcerated because their lack of control makes them easy to catch.

Psychopaths, however, are calculated criminals. They plan every detail, cover their tracks, and manipulate those around them to shift blame elsewhere. While sociopaths tend to engage in spontaneous crimes of passion, psychopaths are more likely to orchestrate elaborate financial schemes, commit long-term fraud, or execute carefully premeditated acts of violence. Some of history's most infamous serial killers exhibited clear psychopathic tendencies, methodically selecting victims and were able to evade law enforcement for years. Their patience, attention to detail, and lack of emotional attachment make them far more effective—and terrifying—criminals.

While both sociopaths and psychopaths pose risks, psychopaths are often the greater threat due to their ability to blend in, manipulate, and execute long-term plans without detection. A sociopath might cause chaos in their immediate surroundings, harming those closest to them, but a psychopath can deceive, control, and destroy on a much larger scale. Their ability to mask their nature allows them to rise to positions of influence, making them some of the most potentially dangerous individuals in society.

However, the ongoing debate about the distinction between psychopathy and sociopathy raises important questions. Are these two truly separate conditions or merely different expressions of the same disorder? For example, some believe that sociopaths are on the same spectrum, with psychopaths just being more severely disconnected from human emotional experience than sociopaths.

Are psychopaths different from sociopaths, or is this perception shaped by the way we study and define them? Regardless of these debates, one fact remains clear—those who understand their behaviors are better equipped to recognize and protect themselves from manipulative individuals, ensuring they do not fall prey to deception, exploitation, or harm.

Neurological Foundations of Psychopathy

Previously, we examined the distinctions between psychopathy and sociopathy, noting how psychopaths showcase emotional variability combined with a level of behavioral consistency not seen in sociopaths. This consistency often belies the deep-seated physiological aspects that underpin psychopathy, particularly those impacting neurological pathways. Understanding these differences requires a closer look at the brain mechanisms leading to such distinctive emotional and behavioral traits.

Similar to sociopathy, psychopathy is not just a pattern of antisocial behavior—it is deeply rooted in the brain's structure and function. Decades of neuroscientific research suggest that psychopaths exhibit consistent neurological abnormalities, particularly in regions associated with emotion regulation, impulse control, and moral decision-making (Johanson et al., 2020). These neurological differences offer insight into why psychopaths lack empathy, display callousness, and engage in calculated manipulation without remorse.

The Amygdala and Emotional Processing

One of the most well-documented findings in psychopathy research is reduced activity in the amygdala, the brain region responsible for processing fear, emotions, and social cues. In typical individuals, the amygdala plays a key role in recognizing distress in others, which in turn helps regulate prosocial behavior. However, in psychopaths, this system is impaired.

Similar to sociopaths, neuroimaging studies show that when psychopaths are exposed to images of suffering or pain, their amygdala does not activate in the same way that it does in non-psychopathic individuals (Plackett, 2021). This deficiency explains their inability to empathize with others' pain, making them more likely to manipulate, harm, or exploit without experiencing emotional discomfort.

The Prefrontal Cortex and Impulse Control

Another key region affected in psychopathy is the prefrontal cortex, particularly the orbitofrontal and ventromedial areas. These brain structures are responsible for impulse control, decision-making, and evaluating the consequences of actions. Studies indicate that psychopaths have reduced gray matter volume in these areas, leading to poor impulse regulation and an impaired ability to learn from punishment (Cope et al., 2012). This dysfunction contributes to their tendency to engage in reckless or harmful behaviors without considering long-term repercussions. Unlike sociopaths, whose impulsivity is often driven by emotional instability, psychopaths' impulsivity tends to be more calculated—an expression of their inability to foresee or care about consequences.

The Default Mode Network and Moral Reasoning

Dysfunction in the default mode network (DMN), which serves as the brain's system for introspection, moral reasoning, and self-referential thought, has been identified as playing a significant role in the development of psychopathy (Whitfield-Gabrieli & Ford, 2012). Individuals with psychopathy exhibit lower connectivity within these neural networks, suggesting a fundamental impairment in both self-awareness and moral judgment. This neurological deficit likely contributes to the challenges psychopaths face regarding concepts such as guilt, responsibility, and adherence to social norms.

As a consequence, these individuals often find themselves able to engage in manipulation and deceit without experiencing the internal conflict that typically accompanies such actions among those with a more integrated moral compass. This disconnection from moral reasoning further underscores the complexities of psychopathy and its implications for interpersonal relationships and societal interactions.

Neurotransmitter Imbalances and Risk-Taking

Beyond brain structure, abnormalities in neurotransmitter systems also play a role in psychopathy. Research suggests that psychopaths have lower levels of serotonin, a neurotransmitter linked to impulse control and aggression regulation, and heightened levels of dopamine, which fuels reward-seeking behavior (Corbit et al., 2019). This imbalance may contribute to their sensation-seeking tendencies, driving them toward risky behaviors without fear of negative consequences.

While these neurological findings suggest a biological basis for psychopathy, it's important to keep in mind that not every individual with these brain abnormalities develops into a psychopath, and environmental factors such as childhood experiences, trauma, and social conditioning still play a role in shaping behavior. However, understanding the neurological underpinnings of psychopathy provides insights into why these individuals think and act differently, reinforcing the notion that psychopathy is more than just a moral failing—it is a condition deeply embedded in the brain's wiring.

Activating Psychopathic Tendencies: Environmental Conditions and Trauma

While psychopathy has strong neurological underpinnings, it is not considered to be solely a product of genetics or brain abnormalities. Various environmental factors—such as severe childhood trauma, neglect, abuse, and social conditioning—play a significant role in shaping how psychopathic tendencies manifest.

Not everyone with the neurological markers of psychopathy develops into a full-fledged psychopath; in many cases, early life experiences determine whether these predispositions remain dormant or are activated (Hunter, 2010).

Early Childhood Trauma and Emotional Numbness

Many psychopaths have histories of severe childhood trauma, including physical, emotional, or sexual abuse. Repeated exposure to extreme stress during formative years can lead to emotional numbing, a defense mechanism where the child learns to suppress fear and empathy to survive (Cruz et al., 2022). Over time, this numbing can evolve into callousness, making it easier for the individual to manipulate, harm, or exploit others without remorse.

Children exposed to chronic violence or instability may also become desensitized to suffering. If a child learns early on that displays of emotion lead to further harm, they may begin to suppress their natural emotional responses. This emotional suppression, combined with the brain's impaired ability to process fear and social cues, as seen in neurological studies, creates the cold and calculating traits seen in many psychopaths.

Neglect and the Absence of Emotional Bonding

Beyond outright abuse, emotional neglect—such as the absence of nurturing caregivers or inconsistent parental attention—can also contribute to the development of psychopathic traits. Secure attachment in childhood is a large factor in developing empathy and emotional regulation. When a child does not experience consistent caregiving, they may struggle to form deep emotional connections later in life. This detachment can manifest in adulthood as superficial charm, an inability to form lasting relationships, and a disregard for others' emotions.

Neglect can also lead to the early adoption of manipulative behaviors. A child who grows up in an environment where their needs are consistently ignored may learn that deceit, coercion, or charm are the only effective ways to get what they want. Over time, these strategies become ingrained, forming the foundation for the exploitative tendencies seen in many psychopaths (Cruz et al., 2022).

Social Learning and Exposure to Antisocial Role Models

Another major environmental factor in psychopathy is exposure to antisocial behavior during childhood. If a child is raised in an environment where deceit, aggression, or exploitation are normalized, they may internalize these behaviors as acceptable survival strategies. Parents who exhibit narcissistic or psychopathic traits themselves often fail to provide moral guidance, leading to a child who learns to prioritize power and control over emotional connection.

Similarly, growing up in crime-ridden neighborhoods, unstable foster systems, or environments where violence is rewarded can reinforce a lack of empathy and an aggressive worldview. In such cases, the child may adopt a predatory mindset, seeing others as either threats or opportunities for exploitation (Cruz et al., 2022).

The Interaction Between Biology and Environment

Not all individuals who experience trauma or neglect become psychopaths, just as not all individuals with psychopathic brain structures engage in violent or manipulative behavior. The development of full-blown psychopathy typically results from an interaction between genetic predisposition and environmental conditions.

Understanding the role of environmental conditions in psychopathy helps shed light on potential early interventions. While psychopathy itself is difficult to treat, identifying at-risk children—such as those displaying conduct disorders, cruelty to animals, or persistent manipulative tendencies—can allow for early behavioral interventions that might redirect these tendencies toward more constructive outlets (Bjørnebekk, 2021).

By addressing childhood trauma, promoting stable caregiver relationships, and reinforcing prosocial behaviors, society may mitigate the development of dangerous psychopathic traits before they fully take root.

The Hare Psychopathy Checklist (PCL-R)

When it comes to diagnosing and assessing psychopathy, one of the most widely used and respected tools in the field is the Hare Psychopathy Checklist-Revised (PCL-R).

Developed by psychologist Robert Hare, the PCL-R is a structured assessment designed to measure psychopathic traits in individuals, particularly those in forensic and criminal settings. Essentially, it provides a standardized method to evaluate psychopathy by scoring individuals on a range of behavioral and personality characteristics associated with the disorder.

How the PCL-R Works

The PCL-R consists of 20 criteria, each scored on a scale from 0 to 2, where 0 indicates that the trait does not apply to the individual, 1 signifies that the trait applies to some extent, and 2 means that the trait is strongly present. The total score can range from 0 to 40, with a score of 30 or higher typically indicating a clinical level of psychopathy.

The factors the PCL-R assesses are divided into two categories, each representing a different core dimension of psychopathy. These are as follows:

Factor 1: Interpersonal and Affective Traits (Core Personality Traits)

These traits define the emotional and interpersonal aspects of psychopathy, highlighting how individuals manipulate and interact with others.

- **Glibness and Superficial Charm:** Charismatic but insincere, skilled at deception. Psychopaths often appear articulate, engaging, and confident, using charm as a tool to manipulate.

- **Grandiose Sense of Self-Worth:** Exaggerated belief in personal superiority. They see themselves as uniquely special, deserving of admiration and success without effort.

- **Pathological Lying:** Habitual dishonesty, even without necessity. Lies are not just a means to an end but a way of life, often told effortlessly.

- **Manipulativeness:** Using deceit to control and exploit others. Relationships are transactional, with charm and deception used to gain advantage.

- **Lack of Remorse or Guilt:** No emotional response to harming others. They do not experience regret, regardless of the pain they cause.

- **Shallow Affect:** Emotionally superficial and incapable of deep feelings. Expressions of emotion are often exaggerated or feigned rather than genuine.

- **Lack of Empathy:** Indifference to the suffering of others. Other people's pain is irrelevant unless it serves a personal agenda.

- **Failure to Accept Responsibility:** Blaming others or externalizing blame. Even when caught, they rationalize their actions rather than take ownership.

Factor 2: Social Deviance and Antisocial Behavior (Behavioral Patterns)

This factor measures impulsive, irresponsible, and criminal behaviors that characterize psychopathy in action.

- **Need for Stimulation and Proneness to Boredom:** Constantly seeking excitement. A low tolerance for routine or monotony drives reckless or risky behaviors.

- **Parasitic Lifestyle:** Living off others rather than working. Psychopaths often manipulate people into supporting them financially or emotionally. Engaging in diverse types of crimes

- **Poor Behavioral Controls:** Difficulty managing emotions and impulses. Outbursts of anger or aggression are common, often triggered by frustration.

- **Early Behavioral Problems:** Conduct issues before age 13. Many psychopaths show warning signs in childhood, including cruelty, defiance, or deception.

- **Juvenile Delinquency:** Criminal behavior in adolescence. This often includes theft, violence, or rule-breaking without regard for consequences.

- **Irresponsibility:** Failure to meet obligations or commitments. They frequently abandon jobs, relationships, or responsibilities without concern.

- **Impulsivity:** Acting without thinking of consequences. Decisions are made on a whim, often leading to destructive or self-sabotaging actions.

- **Lack of Realistic, Long-Term Goals:** Unrealistic or poorly planned future. They may claim ambitious goals but lack the discipline to pursue them.

- **Revocation of Conditional Release:** Failing to comply with parole or probation. Even when given second chances, they tend to re-offend.

- **Criminal Versatility:** Rather than specializing in one area, they adapt and exploit opportunities across different illegal activities.

The PCL-R is widely used in criminal justice and forensic psychology to assess risk factors for violent behavior, recidivism, and rehabilitation potential. High-scoring individuals are more likely to engage in repeated criminal activity and show little response to traditional rehabilitation methods. The checklist also provides valuable insight into why certain individuals are resistant to emotional bonds, unresponsive to punishment, and skilled at deceiving those around them.

However, the PCL-R is not without controversy. Critics argue that it overemphasizes criminality and does not account for non-criminal psychopaths—such as corporate executives, politicians, or con artists—who do not engage in overtly illegal behavior but still exhibit high levels of psychopathy. Additionally, the reliance on subjective judgment in scoring is noted to potentially lead to inconsistencies in assessment (Martens, 2008).

Despite these critiques, the PCL-R remains one of the most effective tools available for identifying and studying psychopathy and can be incredibly useful for distinguishing between individuals who possess antisocial behaviors and those who exhibit the full profile of a psychopath.

Psychological Tactics Used by Psychopaths

Imagine a world where charming smiles mask dangerous intentions, where individuals with certain brain structures use their neurological traits as the linchpin for manipulative strategies. Reduced fear responses in psychopaths can embolden them, dulling the ethical brakes that halt harmful actions. This unique cocktail of brain structure irregularities plays a significant role in setting the stage for a captivating yet dangerous game: manipulation.

Charm as a Weapon

Psychopaths often harness interpersonal charm to spin a web of deception. They can be disarmingly charismatic, mirroring the emotions, interests, and values of their targets to create a false sense of connection. Their charisma can enchant, making them appear genuine and trustworthy, playing to people's innate need for connection and approval.

This charm is not genuine; it is a carefully constructed act designed to make others feel special, valued, and safe. A psychopath's charm can be highly intoxicating. They may shower their targets with attention, praise, and even flattery, making the victim feel like they've found someone who truly understands them. However, this phase—often referred to as "love bombing" in the context of romantic relationships—is merely a setup for the manipulation that follows.

In social settings, these tactics can manifest as seemingly endless attention, compliments, and a sense of empathy and understanding. Take, for instance, a scenario where a charismatic leader enters a community and earns trust and admiration. Their genuine demeanor can lead to influence, easily disguising self-serving motives under the allure of magnetism. Such charm opens doors, introduces opportunities, and can swiftly trap unsuspecting individuals in a dynamic where power subtly shifts away from them.

Deception and Lying

Psychopaths are pathological liars, but unlike ordinary liars, they lie effortlessly and entirely without guilt. Their ability to weave stories is often unparalleled. They change narratives to suit their needs, demonstrating no typical physiological responses to lying, such as nervous tics or eye aversion. This makes them incredibly persuasive and difficult to expose.

The art of their deception often is the result of presenting lies alongside partial truths, making their tales more believable and harder to dissect. This deception is often subtle and layered, mixing truth with lies so seamlessly that their victims struggle to discern reality. They fabricate elaborate stories about their past, inflate their achievements, or present themselves as victims of injustice to gain sympathy and trust.

Beyond verbal deception, psychopaths wield emotional manipulation to distort and control perceptions. They might feign emotions they don't genuinely feel, such as love, guilt, or compassion, using these emotional displays to exploit the empathetic and nurturing tendencies of others. Such manipulation exploits emotional bonds, using them to redirect behavior in a way that serves the manipulator's interests, all while the manipulated feels like an active participant.

Gaslighting and Reality Manipulation

Gaslighting is a psychological warfare tactic psychopaths use to make their victims question their own perceptions and reality. By denying things they have said or done, twisting the truth, or accusing the victim of being overly sensitive or paranoid, they create an environment where their target becomes unsure of their own memories and judgment.

Over time, the victim may begin to rely entirely on the psychopath for guidance on what is "true" or "real," making them more vulnerable to further exploitation. Gaslighting can be subtle, such as dismissing someone's concerns as irrational, or extreme, such as rewriting history to make the victim doubt their own sanity.

Isolation techniques present another insidious strategy. By slowly eroding a person's social connections, psychopaths can ensure their influence remains unrivaled. They may sow seeds of distrust, create conflict within social groups, or monopolize a person's time and attention, leading to the gradual stripping away of supportive social networks. This leaves the victim far more vulnerable to reality distortion, with limited perspectives outside the manipulator's influence.

Baiting and Provoking Emotional Reactions

Psychopaths are skilled at pushing people's buttons to provoke emotional responses. They might intentionally insult, belittle, or humiliate their victims just to see how they react. Once the victim becomes emotional—whether through anger, frustration, or sadness—the psychopath turns the situation against them, painting them as unstable or irrational.

This tactic serves two purposes: it allows the psychopath to maintain control over the situation while simultaneously making their victim doubt their own emotions and reactions. If they can convince the victim that they are overly sensitive or prone to overreacting, future manipulation will be even easier.

While reviewing the behaviors can be unnerving, clearly recognizing these tactics can be an incredible defense. Awareness allows for stronger personal boundaries and can help individuals better identify dangerous individuals and act accordingly. Understanding how charm, deceit, emotional manipulation, and isolation can be wielded against us helps build resilience against insidious influence and ensures that our decisions and lives remain firmly in our hands, not puppeteered by the manipulation of a psychopath.

Case Study: Corporate Predator

In the sleek, glass-walled headquarters of a multimillion-dollar corporation, Daniel Kessler sat at the top of the hierarchy—ruthless, charismatic, and feared. From the outside, he was the epitome of success: a self-made entrepreneur with an uncanny ability to close deals and a reputation for turning struggling companies into profit machines. But beneath the polished exterior was a man devoid of conscience, whose hunger for power and control left a wake of destruction in his path.

Kessler's early career was marked by an almost supernatural ability to manipulate those around him. He knew exactly how to charm investors, dazzle the media, and persuade employees to follow his vision with unwavering loyalty. His words were smooth, his confidence unwavering—he could make anyone believe he was their greatest ally.

But those who worked closely with him soon learned that his charm was merely a tool, a mask he wore to get what he wanted.

Early in his tenure as CEO, he implemented cutthroat policies that increased profits at the expense of his employees' well-being. He deliberately pitted colleagues against each other, creating a toxic environment where paranoia thrived. Kessler would single out employees for public humiliation, using their mistakes—real or fabricated—to instill fear. Those who questioned him were swiftly discarded, their careers shattered. Yet, he always maintained plausible deniability, ensuring that any scandal or failure could be pinned on someone else.

Kessler's psychopathy was most evident in how he treated people as disposable resources. He identified vulnerabilities in others and exploited them without hesitation. A talented but insecure executive became his most loyal subordinate after Kessler convinced him that only his leadership could bring out his full potential. A junior employee struggling financially was subtly coerced into unethical practices to "prove" his commitment to the company.

His lack of empathy was particularly chilling in moments of crisis. When a long-time employee died suddenly from stress-related heart failure, Kessler offered no condolences—only a curt remark about finding a replacement. When layoffs were necessary, he relished the power he had over people's livelihoods, often delivering the news with a smirk or a dismissive wave.

Despite his ability to deceive, Kessler's reckless pursuit of power eventually led to his downfall. Investors began questioning discrepancies in financial reports, and employees—driven to the brink—started speaking out. Whistleblowers came forward, revealing fraudulent practices, workplace abuse, and even illegal intimidation tactics.

In a dramatic corporate scandal, Kessler was ousted from his position, his carefully constructed empire crumbling overnight. He faced charges of financial misconduct, but true to his nature, he denied all responsibility. Even as his empire fell, he remained unshaken, convinced he would manipulate his way back to the top.

Concluding Thoughts

Understanding the neurological and psychological aspects of psychopathy allows us to confront the profound complexities surrounding these antisocial traits. By distinguishing the unique characteristics of psychopathy from sociopathy, we gain vital insights into emotional detachment and behavioral consistency that significantly impact personal safety and interpersonal relationships.

Recognizing the specific neurological underpinnings, such as the amygdala and prefrontal cortex's role in emotional regulation and decision-making, equips us with the knowledge to identify psychopathic behaviors better. This awareness is crucial for safeguarding against manipulation and developing effective strategies for engagement, treatment, and prevention.

As we move forward, this understanding empowers professionals and the general public alike to anticipate potential threats, enhance mental health interventions, and promote healthier interactions within diverse environments. With these revelations, we can build more informed and resilient communities equipped to handle the challenges posed by psychopathic tendencies with greater confidence and empathy.

Chapter 4:

DSM-V Demystified—Identifying the Criminal Mind Clinically

As the morning sun slipped through the blinds, Detective Hall leaned back in his chair, studying the case file spread across his desk. The suspect's record was as long as it was disturbing—each entry a testament to both a disregard for rules and an uncanny ability to evade consequences. Hall also noted a chilling pattern: each crime—theft, deceit, aggression—was all executed with a brazen confidence that seemed almost natural. This wasn't just lawbreaking; it was a lifestyle, one that seemed to be rooted in something much more sinister. As he reviewed the details, Hall found himself wondering, *"What could drive a person to rewrite their own moral code so effortlessly?"*

Criminal behavior can be deeply puzzling to most law-abiding citizens, and the reckless disregard for others that often accompanies it is mystifying. In this chapter, we'll take a closer look at the DSM-V criteria used to identify antisocial behavior disorders and the assessment methods that help identify individuals likely to commit crimes or engage in harmful behavior, such as sociopaths and psychopaths.

The ultimate goal is to equip you with deeper insights that can help you identify these individuals and avoid falling victim to their manipulation.

DSM-V Criteria

The *Diagnostic and Statistical Manual of Mental Disorders, Fifth Edition* (DSM-V) serves as the primary reference for mental health professionals diagnosing a range of psychiatric conditions. Its primary function is to provide standardized criteria for each disorder, ensuring consistency across clinical settings. However, the DSM-V does not account for every nuance of human behavior—diagnoses are made based on observed patterns of thoughts, emotions, and behaviors that cause distress or impairment.

As introduced in Chapter 1, antisocial personality disorder (ASPD) is one such diagnosis. It falls under Cluster B personality disorders, which are characterized by dramatic, emotional, or erratic behaviors. Unlike conditions such as anxiety or depression, which fluctuate over time, personality disorders represent deeply ingrained patterns of relating to the world. ASPD is particularly controversial because it describes individuals who engage in chronic manipulation, deceit, and exploitation, often with little remorse.

While the DSM-V does not officially recognize psychopathy as a distinct disorder, ASPD is the closest clinical equivalent. However, many experts argue that ASPD and psychopathy, though overlapping, are not identical—psychopathy is often assessed using the Hare Psychopathy Checklist-Revised (PCL-R) rather than the DSM-V. Below, we break down ASPD's criteria, followed by a comparison with psychopathy and sociopathy.

Diagnostic Criteria: A Quick Recap of Antisocial Personality Disorder (ASPD)

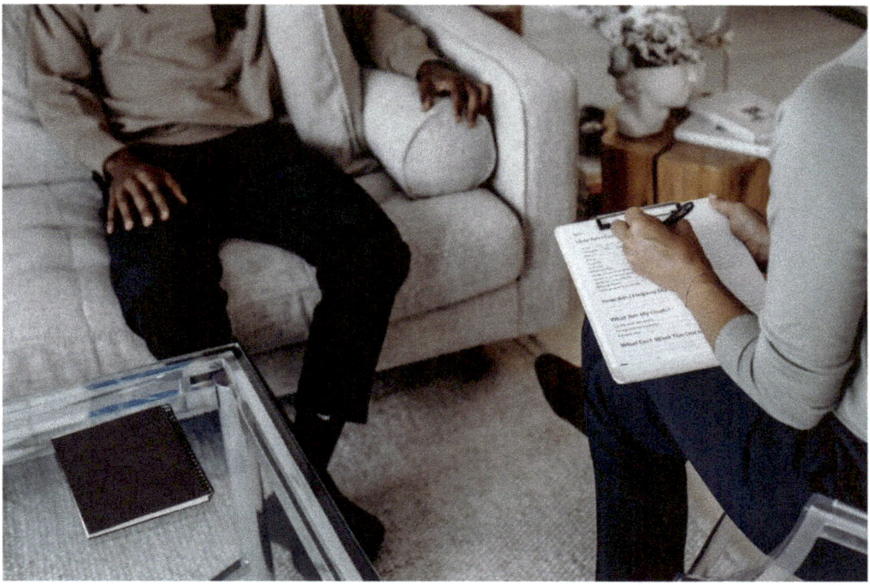

To receive a diagnosis of antisocial personality disorder (ASPD), an individual must exhibit a "pervasive pattern of disregard for and violation of the rights of others," beginning by age 15 and demonstrated by at least three of the following behaviors (American Psychiatric Association, 2013).

- Failure to conform to social norms with respect to lawful behaviors, engaging in repeated criminal acts such as theft, fraud, or physical violence.

- Deceitfulness, characterized by repeated lying, use of aliases, or conning others for personal profit or pleasure.

- Impulsivity, making reckless decisions without forethought or consideration of consequences.

- Aggression and irritability, often manifesting as repeated physical fights or assaults.

- Reckless disregard for the safety of self or others, engaging in risky behaviors such as reckless driving or dangerous thrill-seeking with little concern for potential harm.

- A persistent pattern of irresponsibility, including failure to sustain consistent work behavior or honor financial obligations.

- A lack of remorse, showing indifference to or rationalization of having hurt, mistreated, or stolen from another.

Beyond these behavioral patterns, the DSM-V specifies additional criteria to differentiate ASPD from other conditions. The individual must be at least 18 years old at the time of diagnosis, as personality traits evolve over time and cannot be conclusively diagnosed in minors. There also must be evidence of conduct disorder before age 15, a childhood condition characterized by aggression toward people or animals, destruction of property, deceitfulness, and serious rule violations.

Additionally, the antisocial behavior must not be "exclusively during the course of schizophrenia or bipolar disorder," ensuring that the traits are not secondary to another psychiatric condition (American Psychiatric Association, 2013).

Psychopathy, Sociopathy, and Subsets of Clinical Antisocial Personality Disorder

As outlined in earlier chapters, psychopathy and sociopathy are often referenced as distinct subtypes within the broader diagnosis of ASPD. While the DSM-V does not officially categorize ASPD into these subtypes, understanding these variations through the lens of the DSM-V can help differentiate how antisocial traits manifest.

Psychopathy, as measured by the Hare Psychopathy Checklist-Revised (PCL-R), is considered a more extreme and specific manifestation of ASPD. In essence, all psychopaths meet the criteria for ASPD, but not everyone with ASPD is severe enough to qualify as a psychopath.

Compared to general ASPD, psychopathy is marked by severe callousness, complete emotional detachment, and a high degree of manipulation. Individuals with psychopathy tend to be calculated and charming rather than impulsive and reactive, using their charisma to deceive and exploit others. This detachment often results in a preference for premeditated crimes rather than impulsive acts of violence, making psychopaths particularly dangerous.

Sociopathy, though not an official clinical term, is often used to describe a more impulsive and emotionally volatile form of ASPD. Unlike psychopaths, who tend to be cold and calculated, sociopaths are prone to outbursts of rage, recklessness, and erratic decision-making. Their disregard for social norms is more reactive than strategic—they may lash out unpredictably rather than manipulate others in a calculated manner.

Sociopaths differ from psychopaths in their ability to form attachments. While psychopaths lack emotional depth and struggle to bond with others, sociopaths may develop attachments to select individuals, though these relationships are often dysfunctional and unstable. Their impulsivity and difficulty regulating emotions frequently lead to substance abuse, physical violence, and chaotic lifestyles (Haghighi, 2021).

Diagnostic Controversies

Diagnosing ASPD presents unique challenges, both in clinical and forensic settings. The disorder is deeply tied to behavioral patterns rather than subjective distress, which makes assessment difficult—particularly when individuals may have incentives to either exaggerate or conceal their traits.

Additionally, the ethical implications of labeling someone as "antisocial" or "psychopathic" raise concerns about bias, stigma, and the potential misuse of psychiatric diagnoses in legal and institutional settings.

Overdiagnosis vs. Underdiagnosis

A major debate in psychology and psychiatry is whether ASPD is overdiagnosed. On one hand, the disorder is often associated with criminal behavior, and some argue that it is too easily applied to individuals with histories of aggression, delinquency, or substance abuse without thorough psychological evaluation.

In forensic settings, where ASPD diagnoses can impact sentencing or parole decisions, there is concern that individuals may be mislabeled based on past actions rather than a true personality disorder (Aharoni et al., 2022).

Conversely, some clinicians believe ASPD is underdiagnosed, especially in high-functioning individuals who evade legal consequences (Balsis et al., 2007). Many people with ASPD, particularly those who exhibit psychopathic traits, are adept at avoiding detection by maintaining a superficial charm or manipulating others into dismissing their antisocial behaviors. This means that individuals who pose a genuine risk may not receive a formal diagnosis until after they have already caused significant harm.

The Ethics of Labeling: Legal and Social Consequences

Applying labels such as "psychopath" or "antisocial" carries significant ethical weight. These terms are often associated with dangerousness and criminality, leading to potential biases in the legal system, healthcare, and even social interactions. Once an individual is diagnosed with ASPD, they may face lifelong stigma, limited access to rehabilitation programs, and difficulty reintegrating into society.

In criminal justice settings, the diagnosis can also be misused. For example, a label of psychopathy, based on tools like the PCL-R, can influence parole boards or sentencing decisions, potentially leading to harsher treatment even when an individual has shown no recent violent tendencies. Conversely, some may argue that failing to diagnose and recognize ASPD early can allow dangerous individuals to manipulate systems and re-offend without intervention.

Perhaps the most controversial question in ASPD research is whether the disorder can be treated or if it represents a permanent and unchangeable condition. Traditional therapy approaches, which rely on developing insight and emotional connection, often fail with individuals who lack empathy and have little motivation to change. Some studies suggest that therapy may even make some individuals with ASPD more manipulative, as they learn new psychological tactics to exploit others (Flaaten et al., 2024).

Clinical Assessment Techniques

In a clinical setting, interviews are a crucial first step in diagnosing ASPD. These interviews help clinicians evaluate an individual's history, behavioral patterns, and emotional responses. However, because individuals with ASPD are often deceptive or manipulative, clinicians cannot rely solely on self-reported symptoms. Instead, they employ structured interviews, psychological testing, and real-world behavioral observations to gather a more accurate picture of an individual's personality and behavioral patterns.

Common questions that can be used to assess ASPD traits include:

- Have you ever done something illegal and not felt guilty about it? (Assessing lack of remorse)
- Do you find it easy to manipulate others to get what you want? (Evaluating deceitfulness)
- Do you tend to act without thinking about the consequences? (Measuring impulsivity)

Since individuals with ASPD may lie or minimize their behaviors, clinicians often compare their responses to collateral information from past legal records, employment history, or reports from family members.

Psychological Testing: Objective Tools for Diagnosis

Psychological tests provide measurable data to supplement clinical interviews. These tests help differentiate ASPD from other disorders and assess the severity of antisocial traits. In addition to the PCL-R we reviewed in the previous chapter, which is specific to diagnosing psychopathic tendencies, the following assessments are often used:

- **The Minnesota Multiphasic Personality Inventory-2 (MMPI-2)**: This comprehensive personality test includes scales that measure antisocial traits, impulsivity, aggression, and emotional detachment. Certain MMPI-2 profiles, particularly elevations in the Psychopathic Deviate (Pd) scale, can indicate ASPD tendencies (Floyd & Gupta, 2023).

- **Structured Clinical Interview for DSM-V Personality Disorders (SCID-II/SCID-5-PD)**: A formal diagnostic tool that evaluates all major personality disorders, including ASPD, by systematically assessing symptoms such as chronic violation of the law, deceitfulness, impulsivity, irritability, aggression, and lack of remorse against DSM-V criteria (First et al., 2018).

Behavioral Observations: Assessing Antisocial Personality Disorder in Real-World Contexts

Since individuals with ASPD are often manipulative and untruthful in clinical settings, behavioral observations play a key role in diagnosis. Trained professionals assess how an individual behaves in real-world situations, particularly under stress or scrutiny.

- **Prison Interviews and Forensic Evaluations**: In correctional facilities, professionals observe inmates for patterns of deceit, aggression, and lack of remorse. Some individuals with ASPD will present as charming and cooperative, while others display outright hostility.

- **Courtroom Behavior**: Judges, attorneys, and forensic psychologists note how a defendant interacts with authority figures, their ability to feign remorse, and whether they attempt to manipulate legal proceedings to their advantage.

- **Therapy Sessions**: Even when seeking treatment, individuals with ASPD may test boundaries, lie about their experiences, or attempt to exploit the therapist. Clinicians look for signs such as an inability to form genuine emotional connections or a consistent failure to take responsibility for past actions.

Understanding Co-morbidities in Antisocial Personality Disorder

Antisocial personality disorder rarely exists in isolation. Many individuals diagnosed with ASPD also exhibit traits of other psychiatric conditions, a phenomenon known as co-morbidity. These overlapping disorders can complicate diagnosis and treatment, often intensifying antisocial behaviors and making rehabilitation even more challenging.

The most common co-occurring conditions include substance use disorders (SUDs), narcissistic personality disorder (NPD), and borderline personality disorder (BPD). Understanding these co-morbidities provides deeper insight into the complexity of the criminal mind (Fisher et al., 2024).

Substance Abuse and Antisocial Personality Disorder: A Dangerous Reinforcement Loop

Substance use disorders are one of the most frequent co-morbidities in individuals with ASPD. Studies indicate that a large percentage of individuals with ASPD struggle with drug or alcohol addiction, often using substances to heighten their impulsivity or suppress emotional discomfort (Moeller & Dougherty, 2024).

- **Impulsivity and risk-taking:** Individuals with ASPD already display reckless, thrill-seeking behaviors. Drug use, particularly stimulants like cocaine or methamphetamine, exacerbates this impulsivity, making them even more prone to criminal activity and violence.

- **Lack of remorse and substance use**: Many individuals with ASPD feel little guilt about the consequences of their actions. They may steal, manipulate, or engage in violent acts to obtain drugs without concern for others.

- **Treatment challenges**: Traditional addiction recovery programs rely on introspection, accountability, and emotional connection—qualities that are often underdeveloped in individuals with ASPD. This makes rehabilitation efforts particularly difficult, as they may manipulate treatment providers rather than engage sincerely in recovery.

Antisocial Personality Disorder and Narcissistic Personality Disorder (NPD)

Narcissistic personality disorder (NPD) and ASPD frequently overlap, creating a particularly exploitative and grandiose individual. While not all people with ASPD are narcissistic, those with both disorders tend to be among the most manipulative and socially destructive.

Key similarities between ASPD and NPD include a lack of empathy, a disregard for others, and a willingness to exploit people for personal gain. However, there are key differences: narcissists crave admiration and validation, while individuals with ASPD may not place the same importance on social status; for them, control and power are what truly matter.

When these disorders coexist, individuals may become extremely manipulative, exhibiting high levels of charisma, persuasion, and deceitfulness, making them capable of orchestrating large-scale frauds, corporate scams, or emotionally abusive relationships with chilling ease. Some forensic experts speculate that many high-functioning psychopaths display strong narcissistic traits, making them particularly dangerous in corporate and political settings.

Antisocial Personality Disorder and Borderline Personality Disorder (BPD)

Borderline Personality Disorder (BPD) is a condition characterized by intense mood swings, fear of abandonment, and emotional outbursts. Though ASPD and BPD may initially seem like opposite disorders—one marked by emotional detachment, the other by emotional instability—they frequently co-occur, particularly in individuals with severe childhood trauma or neglect. When combined, individuals may oscillate between extreme aggression and desperate emotional pleas, often using both as manipulation tactics.

Furthermore, both disorders involve poor impulse control, making affected individuals prone to dangerous behaviors, including substance abuse, reckless driving, or violent altercations. Those with co-occurring BPD and ASPD often experience turbulent personal relationships characterized by cycles of emotional manipulation, violence, and self-destruction. In forensic settings, these individuals may be responsible for particularly erratic crimes, sometimes blending moments of remorse with extreme aggression.

Case Study: The Charming Drifter

Ethan had been drifting from city to city for most of his adult life, leaving behind a trail of broken relationships, unpaid debts, and unanswered questions. Born into a middle-class family, he exhibited troubling behaviors from an early age—petty theft, chronic lying, and an unsettling lack of emotional connection to those around him. Teachers described him as "intelligent but disruptive," while his parents alternated between frustration and denial. By the time he was 14, he had already been expelled from two schools and arrested for vandalism.

Diagnosed with conduct disorder as a teenager, Ethan's behavior only escalated. He was quick to charm authority figures, convincing school counselors that he was misunderstood while manipulating peers into taking the blame for his actions. At 18, he left home without a word, embarking on a transient lifestyle that would define the next two decades of his life.

Ethan's defining trait was his ability to shape-shift. He could be whoever someone needed him to be—an ambitious entrepreneur, a struggling artist, a war veteran with unseen scars. In reality, he had no real career, no stable home, and no intention of changing. Instead, he survived by conning his way into financial and emotional support, often targeting empathetic individuals who believed they could help him.

Ethan's Deceptions in Therapy

Between the ages of 25 and 40, Ethan sought therapy multiple times but not for personal growth. Instead, he used the sessions as a stage, testing how convincingly he could fabricate trauma and remorse.

During his first documented psychological evaluation, Ethan claimed to have suffered from severe childhood abuse, complete with intricate yet inconsistent details. His therapist, moved by his apparent pain, advocated for him to receive housing assistance and social services. Once approved, Ethan disappeared without a trace, only to repeat the process months later in a different city.

After a brief stint in jail for fraud, Ethan entered therapy again, this time as part of a mandated program. Here, he presented himself as an eager participant, quoting psychological jargon and feigning self-awareness. He even volunteered for a university study on personality disorders, charming researchers into believing he was making progress. His participation ended abruptly when inconsistencies in his self-reported history raised red flags.

By his late 30s, Ethan's deception was more refined. When confronted with contradictions in his narrative, he pivoted effortlessly, blaming memory lapses or dissociative episodes. His ability to mimic genuine introspection made it difficult for even experienced clinicians to determine what was real and what was manipulation.

Assessment and Outcome

After multiple encounters with the mental health system, Ethan was formally assessed using the PCL-R, where he scored alarmingly high in key psychopathic traits. His glibness and superficial charm were notable; therapists observed that he could be incredibly engaging, weaving compelling stories that created an illusion of vulnerability and misunderstanding. This charm was often coupled with pathological lying, as he frequently contradicted himself but did so with such confidence that his inconsistencies were often overlooked.

Additionally, Ethan demonstrated a profound lack of remorse or guilt. When questioned about those he had manipulated, he expressed no genuine regret, only frustration at being caught. His lifestyle reflected a parasitic nature as he relied on deception to secure financial support instead of maintaining a steady job, often posing as someone in need to elicit sympathy.

His impulsivity and irresponsibility further characterized his behavior; he made reckless decisions without any concern for the consequences, leaving therapists, friends, and partners to deal with the aftermath of his actions.

Ultimately, Ethan was diagnosed with ASPD, with strong psychopathic tendencies. The clinicians who assessed him recognized that therapy had never served as a means of self-improvement for him; instead, it was merely another stage for his performance.

Ethan's case highlights the profound challenges in treating individuals with ASPD, particularly those who exhibit psychopathic traits. His ability to deceive even seasoned professionals underscores the limitations of traditional therapy when faced with manipulative individuals who have no true desire to change.

While some individuals with ASPD show responsiveness to structured interventions, Ethan remained uninterested in any form of accountability or rehabilitation. To him, therapy was just another con—a game to be played and won.

Clinical Challenges

By understanding the traits and behaviors associated with antisocial disorders, alongside the diagnostic criteria and assessments used to clinically identify these individuals, we gain the ability to spot patterns that might otherwise go unnoticed, which makes us more able to be vigilant in our own lives. Knowledge is protection. It allows us to set boundaries, make informed choices, and, ultimately, avoid becoming entangled in harmful dynamics.

However, awareness doesn't stop at recognizing psychological criteria or deceptive behavioral patterns as they occur. The next chapter will shift into how we might identify the red flags and early warning signs of dangerous individuals as they might manifest in our ordinary social interactions. How do you recognize manipulation in a conversation? What subtle cues can reveal a lack of empathy? And perhaps most importantly, how can you learn to trust your instincts when something feels *off*?

Chapter 5:

Recognizing the Warning Signs—Early Identification of Criminal Minds

In a small, tight-knit community, Sarah was known for her charisma and enthusiasm. She had an infectious laugh that could lighten any room and an open-door policy for friends and neighbors alike. Yet, beneath her welcoming demeanor, those closest to her observed subtle inconsistencies. For instance, there were times when her lively conversations would suddenly give way to sharp remarks or an unexplainable coldness, like a switch had been flipped. However, those moments were typically fleeting, and she'd switch the charm back on quickly, so they often went unnoticed.

Sarah's behavior also included moments where empathy seemed absent. Like the day her friend shared devastating personal news and Sarah responded with indifference, quickly changing the subject back to herself. Her ability to project charisma often masked this lack of connection, leaving those around her puzzled rather than alarmed. Yet, as this pattern of unexpected callousness and hostility grew more pronounced, questions arose in her social circles.

While Sarah's behavior might not immediately raise alarms, it exemplifies a pattern often seen in individuals with antisocial tendencies. The shift from ordinary to ominous is rarely sudden. It creeps in quietly—a lingering glance that holds too long, a casual joke laced with something darker, an intuition that something is off that we can't quite place. It can be reassuring to tell ourselves that malevolence will wear a mask we can recognize, that the dangerous ones among us stand apart, visibly marked by their intentions. But history, both personal and collective, tells a different story.

In this chapter, we'll begin to sharpen our perceptions, not just to understand the behaviors and traits of the dangerous individuals among us but to recognize the early signs and red flags, not in hindsight but in real time. Because the sooner we recognize the warning signs, the sooner we can act.

Early Indicators and Red Flags

Danger does not always announce itself with a raised voice or a clenched fist. More often, it arrives as a whisper—a fleeting moment of discomfort, a barely perceptible shift in tone, an interaction that lingers in the mind for reasons that seem irrational.

The earliest warning signs of antisocial behavior are subtle, frequently dismissed as quirks, misunderstandings, or social awkwardness. But these moments, when viewed as a larger pattern, can be revealing. Recognizing them early and acting with vigilance can be the difference between safe avoidance and irreversible entanglement with a harmful individual.

As we explored in the previous chapter, the DSM-V defines a range of behaviors characteristic of antisocial personality disorder (ASPD), including persistent disregard for others' rights, impulsivity, deceitfulness, and lack of remorse. However, these traits don't always present as overt aggression or violence. In fact, many individuals with sociopathic or psychopathic tendencies are highly skilled at blending in. They do not overstep boundaries or break rules immediately—they test them.

As such, early signs often fall outside what we traditionally think of as dangerous. They might manifest as a slight mismatch between words and actions, an unusual level of confidence in a stranger, or a moment where your instincts tug at you, warning you without concrete proof.

These signs are easily rationalized away, which is precisely why they work. In fact, many of the early warning signs of sociopaths and psychopaths are disguised as charisma, humor, or harmless boundary-pushing. Below are some of the subtle indicators:

- **Microexpressions of Contempt or Disdain**: A flicker of irritation or amusement at someone else's discomfort, quickly masked by a smile. Unlike normal human expressions, which flow naturally, these are out of place—lingering just a second too long before being consciously adjusted.

- **Excessive Familiarity Too Soon:** Some people are naturally warm and open, but those with antisocial tendencies use premature intimacy as a strategy. They may offer personal details to manufacture a sense of trust or touch on deeper topics before a natural rapport has formed. This creates a false sense of connection, lowering defenses.

- **Boundary Testing Through Small Violations:** They start with trivial transgressions: borrowing an item and "forgetting" to return it, playfully teasing in a way that feels slightly too pointed, or standing just a little too close in conversation. These minor acts serve as probes—seeing what they can get away with and whether the other person will push back.

- **Mismatched Emotional Reactions:** Someone tells a sad story, and instead of sympathy, there's amusement. A tense situation arises, and they remain eerily calm. Their reactions to emotionally charged moments feel off, as though they are mimicking expected responses rather than truly feeling them.

- **Superficial Charm:** They say all the right things but in a way that feels rehearsed. Compliments come too easily, laughter seems calculated, and the charm, while effective, lacks warmth or authenticity. It's engagement without depth—connection without sincerity.

Escalation Patterns: From Minor Rule-Breaking to Criminal Acts

People with antisocial tendencies typically do not immediately reveal their full nature. Instead, their behaviors progress in a series of escalating steps, each one normalizing the next (Anderson & Kiehl, 2014). Early-stage rule-breaking often looks like:

- **Flouting Social Norms**: Cutting in line, subtly mocking authority figures, disregarding minor social conventions—not in an overtly rebellious way, but with a quiet amusement, as if the rules don't apply to them.

- **Pushing Moral Boundaries in Conversation**: Joking about unethical behavior, downplaying harm, or casually mentioning past actions that seem inconsiderate or cruel. These comments often come disguised as humor, testing whether others will challenge or condone them.

- **Dismissal of Consequences**: They talk about getting away with things—parking tickets they never paid, responsibilities they dodged, lies they told without repercussion. The underlying message is always the same: consequences are for other people but shouldn't apply to me.

- **Encouraging Others to Bend the Rules**: Dangerous and manipulative individuals may push those around them to engage in questionable behavior, often in subtle ways—taking shortcuts at work, lying to get ahead, or breaking minor laws. Beyond establishing complicity, this behavior also often serves a large purpose: gauging how easily someone can be influenced.

These early behaviors, while often of limited impact, set the stage for deeper manipulation. By the time they escalate—whether into fraud, abuse, or violence—we've often been conditioned to second-guess our instincts or accept small wrongs as normal.

Of added influence is the fact that most people are conditioned to give others the benefit of the doubt. We typically assume that odd moments are misunderstandings, that small violations are accidental, and that charm equates to good intentions. But those who exploit others rely on this—our socialized reluctance to trust our own discomfort and instincts can leave us vulnerable.

The earliest warning signs are often not dramatic. They are quiet inconsistencies, moments that don't add up, subtle shifts that set off something deep in the gut. And that is exactly why they are so dangerous. The key is to find a balance, pattern recognition, and vigilance without outright paranoia. One strange moment might mean nothing. But when the same unease arises again and again, it's worth paying attention to other warning signs.

Exploitation of Social Norms

Society runs on unspoken rules—assumptions of goodwill, politeness, and reciprocity. Most people follow these norms without question, trusting that others will do the same. But individuals with antisocial traits—particularly sociopaths and psychopaths—see these rules not as moral guidelines but as weaknesses to be used to their advantage. They manipulate the invisible framework of social expectations, pushing limits while ensuring their actions appear justifiable or harmless.

The most dangerous aspect of this exploitation is that it often goes unnoticed. These individuals don't break the rules outright; they bend them in ways that make resistance feel awkward or socially costly. Because these tactics are subtle and work within existing social norms rather than against them, by the time they are exposed, the damage is often already done.

Using Charm and Deception to Gain Trust

Charm is often the first avenue of deception for antisocial and manipulative individuals. They present as warm, engaging, and deeply attuned to those around them. This isn't a genuine connection but a carefully curated persona designed to prevent suspicion. Often, they mirror the interests and speech patterns of the person they're targeting, creating an illusion of familiarity.

At times, they manufacture a sense of shared vulnerability, offering up personal hardships—real or fabricated—to encourage emotional intimacy. Small acts of kindness, well-placed compliments, or exaggerated enthusiasm lower defenses further, making their motives harder to question and overall making them come across as trustworthy.

Testing Boundaries Through Small Transgressions

Early in an interaction, dangerous individuals begin testing boundaries in subtle, almost imperceptible ways. Rather than violating them outright, they introduce minor infractions to gauge resistance and assess how much they can get away with. A lingering presence in someone's personal space, standing just a little too close for comfort; a touch that seems just a little too familiar, perhaps a hand on the lower back or an unnecessary brush of the arm; a teasing comment that carries an undercurrent of insult disguised as humor—each action is carefully designed to normalize discomfort.

If their target fails to push back, even slightly, the behavior gradually escalates, moving from minor social transgressions to more overt forms of control. They also take note of how a person reacts to a "soft no." If someone expresses reluctance—hesitating before agreeing to something, offering an excuse rather than a firm refusal, or attempting to deflect with humor—but doesn't enforce their boundary, the manipulator interprets this as permission. Rather than yielding to the hesitation of others, they see being able to move beyond it as an invitation to push further the next time.

This gradual conditioning makes it increasingly difficult for the target to recognize when they have been maneuvered into a place of submission or compliance.

Pity and Emotional Goodwill as Manipulation Tactics

Manipulation often takes the form of strategically evoking pity. A well-timed story of betrayal or misfortune encourages sympathy and shifts responsibility onto others. If their behavior is questioned, they blame stress, past trauma, or the misunderstanding of those around them. They may even turn the accusation around, suggesting that their target is being unfair, overreacting, or cruel. Guilt becomes a tool to keep others in line.

A direct challenge to their behavior is met with defensiveness or a sudden display of hurt feelings, making confrontation feel like an act of unnecessary aggression. Look out for inconsistencies in their narratives, emotional outbursts that seem disproportionate to the situation, and manipulation of feelings to deflect accountability.

Developing a healthy skepticism toward these behaviors is the best course of action to prevent exploitation. One doesn't need to be cynical, but balancing empathy with a critical eye can safeguard personal safety. Being aware of one's emotional responses and questioning the motives behind another's actions can serve as an invaluable protective shield.

The Role of Intuition in Early Detection

While society often prioritizes rationality and logic over gut feelings, intuition is an underappreciated yet powerful tool for detecting dangerous or manipulative individuals. Long before clear red flags emerge, the subconscious mind picks up on subtle inconsistencies—tone of voice, microexpressions, or patterns of behavior that don't quite add up. That unease you feel around someone, the inexplicable sense that something is "off," often is not paranoia; it is often an early warning system honed by evolution to detect threats before they become unavoidable.

Manipulative individuals rely on the fact that most people are conditioned to doubt their instincts. They exploit the discomfort their behavior causes by brushing it off as a misunderstanding or even shifting the blame onto the person sensing the threat. This is why self-awareness is crucial—not just in recognizing external warning signs but in trusting one's own reactions to them. A sudden dip in mood when interacting with someone, an uncharacteristic hesitation, or a feeling of being subtly pressured are all signals that should not be ignored.

Awareness also extends beyond the self; observing how a person interacts with others can reveal hidden facets of their character. Do they alter their behavior depending on who they are speaking to? Do they show signs of performative charm—politeness in public but cruelty in private? Are they dismissive of boundaries when they think no one is watching? Not all dangers announce themselves with dramatic displays; many begin as a pattern of small but telling behaviors that, when viewed collectively, reveal the nature of a predator in plain sight.

By combining intuition with conscious awareness, people can learn to identify and sidestep potential threats before they escalate. It is not about living in fear but rather about developing a sharper lens for human behavior—one that prioritizes safety over social conditioning and self-trust over the benefit of the doubt.

Trusting your intuition may seem challenging initially, but it plays a crucial role in building an awareness of potential threats from antisocial individuals. Acknowledging these gut feelings and considering them valid inputs strengthens your ability to navigate complex social situations. Consider the following steps to more fully tune into your intuition when you find yourself feeling that something is off while not able to rationally explain it. Many people have found the following practices useful when trying to make sense of gut feelings:

- **Pause and Acknowledge the Feeling**: When something feels "off," resist the urge to dismiss it immediately. Instead of rationalizing or explaining away your discomfort, take a moment to recognize that your intuition is signaling something worth paying attention to.

- **Identify the Source of Discomfort:** Try to pinpoint what specifically is triggering your unease. Is it their tone, body language, or an inconsistency in their words? Even if you can't articulate a concrete reason, noting these details can help you recognize patterns over time.

- **Observe Their Behavior Over Time:** One isolated incident may not be enough to confirm a person's true intentions, but consistent patterns of boundary pushing, manipulation, or dishonesty should not be ignored. Take note of how they treat others and whether they exhibit different personas in different settings.

- **Test Their Respect for Your Boundaries:** If you're unsure whether someone is violating your space or subtly testing limits, reinforce a small boundary and observe their reaction. A respectful person will acknowledge and adjust, while a manipulative individual may challenge, dismiss, or subtly punish you for asserting yourself.

- **Check in With Your Body's Response:** Pay attention to physical reactions such as tension in your chest, unease in your stomach, or a sudden urge to leave a situation. These bodily cues often register danger before the conscious mind catches up.

- **Seek a Second Perspective:** Discuss your feelings with a trusted friend or family member if you're uncertain about someone's behavior. An outside perspective can provide validation and help confirm whether your intuition is picking up on something real.

- **Give Yourself Permission to Distance:** You don't need definitive proof of someone's harmful intentions to remove yourself from their presence. If interactions with a person consistently make you uncomfortable, trust that feeling and prioritize your own well-being.

- **Practice Self-Trust and Confidence:** The more you listen to your intuition and take action accordingly, the stronger and more reliable it becomes, expanding your overall ability to protect yourself from harm.

If you feel hesitation or doubt when honoring your intuition, try to remind yourself that these instinctual gut feelings are part of an innate skill linked to primal survival. Early humans needed to recognize predators quickly to survive, and though our environment has evolved, this instinct persists.

Our brains and physical responses are still wired to respond to subtle cues. These instinctual judgments can protect us from harm before we recognize a threat. By consciously sharpening your awareness and trusting your instincts, you can enhance your ability to recognize and evade potential dangers early on.

Case Study: Friendly Stranger

It started, as these stories often do, with a smile. Leah, a 31-year-old graphic designer living in a mid-sized city, met Daniel at a local dog park. He complimented her dog, made small talk about the weather, and left her with a warm impression. When she saw him again the next weekend, the conversation picked up easily. He was attentive, funny, and seemed harmless—just a friendly stranger.

Over the next few weeks, Daniel began to appear more often. At first, it felt coincidental—bumping into him at her coffee shop, then later at her gym. He mentioned these meetings as "funny little signs" that they were meant to be friends. Leah, trusting but cautious, kept her distance while remaining polite.

Then, the behavior shifted. Daniel began messaging her on social media, though she hadn't shared her full name or contact details. She was unsettled but tried to convince herself it wasn't a big deal—maybe he'd seen her tagged in a friend's post. She politely replied once, but when the messages continued—escalating from friendly to obsessive—she stopped responding.

That's when he showed up at her apartment building. At first, he stood outside, claiming he was "just in the neighborhood." When she didn't answer his calls or texts, his tone turned darker. Messages flipped from flattery to accusations: "You're ungrateful," "You led me on," "You'll regret this." Leah filed a police report, but with no physical harm or threats, there was little they could do.

The situation spiraled. Daniel left cryptic notes on her car, hacked into one of her online accounts, and even followed her to a friend's house late at night. Leah changed her number, installed cameras, and stayed with family. But Daniel's obsession did not wane—it escalated to breaking into her building and confronting her in the stairwell. Thankfully, a neighbor intervened and called the police. This time, he was arrested.

This case reflects the importance of heeding early warning signs and related social support, especially when an encounter accelerates without consent. Daniel exemplified traits common to individuals with antisocial or obsessive personality traits: charm, persistence, boundary-pushing, and eventual escalation into controlling and violent behavior.

The Value of Early Detection

In understanding the red flags and behavioral indicators of antisocial traits, we gain a powerful toolkit for navigating complex social interactions. Recognizing these signs helps us set firm boundaries and protects us from potential manipulation or harm.

As we become more aware, we transform our instincts into strategic actions, safeguarding not just ourselves but also contributing to healthier and safer environments for those around us. By trusting our intuition and validating our observations with others, we create a network of support that strengthens not only individual safety but collective resilience.

With this knowledge, we are better equipped to foster genuine connections, empower ourselves and others, and cultivate a more informed community that is vigilant against antisocial behaviors.

Chapter 6:

Real-Life Encounters—High-Profile Criminal Cases

Now that we've explored the behaviors, inner workings, and chilling impacts of real-life individuals whose lives exemplify the complex and often terrifying nature of antisocial personality disorder (ASPD) and psychopathy, it's time to take a closer look at real-life examples.

This chapter presents a detailed exploration of the notorious cases of Richard Kuklinski, known as the "Iceman," and Aileen Wuornos, a female serial killer whose life story captured public fascination and horror. Through their distinct backgrounds and heinous crimes, we will examine the psychological profiles that underlie their actions, offering insights into how ASPD manifests in extreme behaviors.

While these true stories may be uncomfortable to read, they illustrate the dire importance of being able to detect dangerous characters in our personal lives and communities.

Case Study: Richard Kuklinski "The Iceman"

Richard Kuklinski, who would later become known as "The Iceman," was born in 1935 in Jersey City, New Jersey, into a deeply dysfunctional and abusive family. His father, Stanley Kuklinski, was a violent alcoholic who regularly beat Richard and his siblings. His mother, Anna, was equally abusive, often resorting to severe corporal punishment in the name of religious discipline.

Violence was an inescapable reality in Kuklinski's childhood, shaping his perception of power, control, and survival. One of the most pivotal moments in his early life was witnessing his father beat his older brother to death. Rather than seeking justice, the family covered up the incident, marking a chilling introduction to the idea that violence could be concealed and consequences avoided. Kuklinski's early environment normalized cruelty and shaped Kuklinski's dark belief that dominance and secrecy were necessary for survival.

Kuklinski was already demonstrating signs of severe antisocial behavior by his youth. He was witnessed torturing and killing neighborhood animals—a well-documented early indicator of psychopathy. As he grew older, his cruelty escalated to crime: burglary, assault, and eventually murder. He committed his first known killing as a teenager, beating a man to death for insulting him.

Rather than experiencing remorse, his ability to kill without hesitation became a defining characteristic, making him an ideal recruit for organized crime. By the 1950s, Kuklinski had attracted the attention of the Gambino crime family, for whom he began working as a contract killer. Unlike many enforcers in the criminal underworld, who were known to be impulsive and unmanaged, he displayed an unsettling level of professionalism and self-control, which allowed him to avoid being caught for years.

He utilized a variety of methods—poison, firearms, strangulation, and even crossbows—to eliminate targets without leaving a trace. His nickname, "The Iceman," stemmed from his practice of freezing victims' bodies to obscure their time of death, making forensic investigations difficult.

Despite his horrific actions in his professional role as a hitman, Kuklinski maintained a double life. To the outside world, he was a loving husband and father, providing for his wife and children in a suburban New Jersey home. He attended family gatherings, participated in neighborhood events, and projected the image of a respectable man. His ability to navigate this façade and even hide his true nature from his wife exemplifies the traits of a highly functioning psychopath adept at manipulating perceptions and creating an illusion of normalcy.

Analysis of Kuklinski's Behavior Through DSM-V Criteria, Sociopathy, and Psychopathy Lenses

The *Diagnostic and Statistical Manual of Mental Disorders* (DSM-V) outlines specific criteria for ASPD, many of which align with Kuklinski's behavior. These include:

- **Deceitfulness and Manipulation:** Kuklinski led a double life, skillfully deceiving those around him, including his own family, about his true nature. He lied effortlessly and adapted his personality depending on the situation.

- **Lack of Remorse:** In interviews, Kuklinski spoke about his killings with a chilling lack of guilt. He described his methods in a matter-of-fact tone, showing no empathy for his victims.

- **Impulsivity and Aggression:** While many of his murders were carefully planned, Kuklinski also committed impulsive acts of violence when he felt disrespected or slighted.

- **Failure to Conform to Social Norms:** Kuklinski defied laws and societal expectations without fear of consequence. He did not experience moral conflict over his actions.

- **Superficial Charm:** Despite his violent tendencies, Kuklinski could be charismatic when necessary, allowing him to blend into society and evade detection for decades.

While ASPD covers a broad range of antisocial behaviors, Kuklinski's traits align most closely with the psychopathy subtype. Unlike sociopaths, who are often erratic and unable to maintain stable lives, psychopaths tend to be more calculated, emotionally detached, and strategic in their actions, which Kuklinski certainly was.

Kuklinski also exemplified the traits of a psychopath through his complete emotional detachment, which allowed him to kill without hesitation, displaying no emotional reaction even when recounting his crimes under interrogation.

Kuklinski's cold calculation was also evident in the meticulous planning of many of his murders, where he experimented with various methods to perfect his craft, even staging some of these crimes to make them appear accidental. Perhaps most notably, his ability to transition seamlessly between the roles of an affectionate father and a ruthless killer illustrates why psychopathy is so dangerous.

Insights: The Deeply Deceptive Nature of Psychopaths

Kuklinski's case provides a stark warning about the deceptive nature of individuals with extreme antisocial traits. His ability to remain undetected for so long underscores a haunting truth: some of the most dangerous people are not the ones who stand out but the ones who blend in almost too well. Yet there were red flags, had someone been looking closely for them.

His demeanor could shift without warning, and those closest to him occasionally sensed something unsettling beneath his calm exterior. People who compartmentalize such darkness often betray themselves in small ways: a sudden flash of aggression, an emotional detachment that feels uncanny, or a secrecy that runs deeper than simple privacy.

Perhaps one of the most telling signs was the absence of genuine emotional responses. Kuklinski, like many with psychopathic traits, could mimic concern or charm when needed, but his reactions often lacked genuine warmth, and his empathy often came across as rehearsed, possessing a somewhat mechanical quality that revealed itself in moments when he was unable to express true connection or vulnerability.

Kuklinski also carefully curated the version of himself he showed to others. He manipulated perceptions, deflected questions, and offered just enough information to seem believable. Those around him may not have known the full story, but many sensed inconsistencies in his lifestyle—unexplained wealth, vague explanations for his absences, and a career that never quite added up. These aren't just quirks; they're often part of a calculated effort to obscure a hidden life.

When faced with individuals like Kuklinski, the most vital defense begins with trust—specifically, trusting one's instincts. When someone consistently responds to serious or emotional events with indifference or polished detachment, it's worth questioning what lies beneath. Many of his victims reported initial feelings of unease, that intangible sense that something was wrong. Intuition, honed by millennia of survival, should never be dismissed outright. If someone feels off, even if there's no tangible evidence, that discomfort deserves further attention.

It's also valuable to watch for patterns rather than isolated incidents. A single lie or manipulative moment might be explainable, but a consistent cycle of deception, control, and emotional coldness signals something far more dangerous and can be determined through observation. Of course, understanding psychological conditions such as antisocial personality disorder or psychopathy that we've learned in early chapters can also make it easier to recognize behavioral cues and patterns otherwise easy to overlook.

Richard Kuklinski's life and crimes offer a disturbing insight into the mind of a high-functioning psychopath. Unlike impulsive criminals who often are caught early, he was deliberate, calculating, and methodical, demonstrating how some of the most dangerous individuals are not the ones who appear openly menacing but those who blend seamlessly into society. His case serves as a stark reminder that true predators often wear masks of normalcy, making awareness and vigilance essential tools for self-protection.

Case Study: Aileen Wuornos "The Damsel of Death"

Aileen Wuornos, one of America's most infamous female serial killers, was born in 1956 in Rochester, Michigan. Her early life was defined by extreme instability and abuse. Abandoned by her teenage mother, Wuornos was left in the care of her grandparents, where she suffered physical and sexual abuse at the hands of her grandfather. Wuornos ran away from home as a teenager, living transiently. By her early adulthood, she was trading sex for food, shelter, or other basic necessities—a form of survival sex work born out of desperation—and had developed a deeply ingrained distrust of men and authority figures.

Her lifestyle and means of survival also exposed her to constant danger, reinforcing the worldview she'd developed as a child, in which violence was both a means of survival and a form of power. She also had numerous run-ins with law enforcement for petty crimes, including theft and disorderly conduct.

Wuornos' criminal behavior would eventually evolve dramatically from petty, nonviolent offenses to egregious acts of premeditated murder. Between 1989 and 1990, she committed a series of shocking killings, taking the lives of several men in Florida.

Probably most chilling was how Wuornos meticulously planned her attacks, often luring her victims with the promise of sex before turning on them ruthlessly, shooting them with a handgun while they were in a vulnerable position, demonstrating a cold, calculated approach devoid of empathy. Each murder showcased her pervasive distrust and belief that these men sought to sexually assault her, an assertion that spiraled into a pattern of unhinged justification for her violent actions.

Wuornos managed to evade capture for an extended period due to several factors. Firstly, she was transient, living a nomadic lifestyle and frequently moving from one place to another, which made it difficult for law enforcement to track her. Additionally, she altered her appearance and used various aliases, helping her to blend into different environments and avoid detection. Her victims were often isolated individuals, such as truck drivers or men seeking companionship, who were less likely to be reported missing immediately.

However, after killing her victims, she would often steal from them, taking their belongings and money, which is what led to her eventual.

arrest in 1991. By the time she was finally caught, she had killed seven men, and in 1992, she was convicted and sentenced to death.

Analysis of Aileen Wuornos' Behavior Through DSM-V Criteria, Sociopathy, and Psychopathy Lenses

Aileen Wuornos exhibited many of the criteria for ASPD throughout her life and criminal behavior, though her presentation diverges significantly from the cold, calculating demeanor often associated with psychopathy.

- **Deceitfulness and Manipulation**: Wuornos frequently fabricated elements of her life story, often shifting narratives about her motives and past. Her accounts of the murders varied across interviews—from self-defense to vengeance—creating confusion about her true intent. Though manipulative, her tactics were often emotionally charged rather than strategic or coolly calculated.

- **Lack of Remorse**: Wuornos did express occasional flashes of remorse, but they were typically interwoven with rage, defensiveness, and blame-shifting. Her outbursts in court and final interviews showed emotional volatility rather than genuine empathy or reflection for the lives she took.

- **Impulsivity and Aggression**: This is one of the most defining traits of Wuornos' behavior. Her killings often occurred during what she described as heated, fearful confrontations. She reacted with deadly force, sometimes preemptively, indicating a low threshold for perceived threats and a highly impulsive response system.

- **Failure to Conform to Social Norms**: Wuornos lived much of her adult life outside the bounds of societal structure—drifting, engaging in sex work, and frequently getting into legal trouble. Her defiance of laws and norms was often a survival mechanism but also reflected a longstanding pattern of antisocial conduct.

- **Irritability and Aggressiveness**: Interviews, courtroom appearances, and interactions with legal authorities all illustrate Wuornos's tendency toward angry outbursts, suspicion, and hostility, even when such behavior jeopardized her own legal standing.

Overall, Wuornos aligned more closely with the sociopathy subtype than psychopathy. Sociopaths are typically more emotionally volatile, prone to reactive aggression, and shaped heavily by their environment. Wuornos' early life was filled with trauma—abandonment, sexual abuse, neglect, and institutionalization—all of which likely contributed to her emotional instability and distrust of others.

Unlike psychopaths, who are often emotionally detached and controlled, Wuornos wore her emotions on the surface. Her rage, paranoia, and desperation were visible in many public interactions. She was often emotionally reactive and impulsive. While she could display superficial charm, it was inconsistent and often laced with sarcasm or bitterness, lacking the polished and calculated demeanor common in psychopaths.

Victims Who Become Predators

Aileen Wuornos's life was not just the story of a serial killer—it was a human tragedy written across decades of abandonment, abuse, and survival on the fringes of society. Her crimes were violent and real, but so too were the forces that shaped her personality.

If Richard Kuklinski's story warns us of hidden predators who wear convincing masks, Wuornos's life is a haunting testament to how untreated trauma and systemic failure can mutate into something equally deadly—and far less predictable.

Unlike those who prey from behind a polished façade, Wuornos's pain was on full display. Her volatility, her paranoia, her mistrust—these weren't concealed. Her pain was raw, often visible, and erratic. Her crimes, horrifying as they were, did not emerge from nowhere. They were the crescendo of a life marked by desperation and unprocessed rage.

Unlike some who manipulate with cold precision, Wuornos oscillated between intense emotion and explosive anger. Those who knew her described her as volatile, paranoid, and quick to feel threatened. But underneath the surface was a woman fraying at the edges—someone who, had she been seen and supported earlier, might never have reached that violent breaking point. Her inability to regulate her emotional state, her mistrust of others, and her view of the world as inherently dangerous were forged in the crucible of lifelong trauma.

For society at large, her case underscores the cost of neglect. The warning signs in Wuornos's case weren't subtle. But Wuornos's case also offers a sobering lesson in personal safety, particularly for the men she ultimately targeted. Her victims were largely strangers—men who picked her up under the assumption of a transactional encounter, often in isolated or vulnerable environments. It highlights the importance of situational awareness. Meeting someone in a vulnerable or private setting—especially someone who appears unstable or highly reactive—calls for caution, no matter their gender or outward appearance.

Aileen Wuornos also challenges traditional perceptions of female criminality, proving that sociopathy and extreme antisocial behavior are not limited by gender. Her case serves as a cautionary tale, illustrating the need to recognize warning signs in individuals who display erratic violence, manipulation, and disregard for human life.

Extreme Cases as Lessons in Vigilance

These stories are more than chilling anecdotes from the margins of human behavior—they are case studies in the consequences of unchecked pathology. Richard Kuklinski and Aileen Wuornos may have operated in different ways, but both reveal how deep-rooted trauma, distorted thinking, and a lack of empathy can culminate in devastating acts of harm and violence. In recalling their stories, we are not glorifying their actions but rather applying them to understand better how we might more readily recognize the warning signs of dangerous individuals.

As we've seen, psychopathy and antisocial personality disorder do not always announce themselves with overt menace. They often emerge in disguise—beneath charm, desperation, or calculated normalcy. And while most individuals with these traits never become killers, their capacity for emotional manipulation, control, and abuse can deeply affect the people around them.

In the next chapter, we'll shift from notorious cases to something far closer to home: the common manipulation and control strategies used by individuals with antisocial tendencies. From gaslighting and guilt-tripping to love bombing and coercion, we'll break down the tactics that often go unnoticed. Understanding these strategies is key to self-protection and building healthier, more vigilant boundaries in our interactions.

Chapter 7:

Manipulation and Control—Strategies of the Criminal Mind

Have you ever met someone whose charm was nearly magnetic, who knew just what to say, how to hold your attention, who made you feel seen and understood, only for something deeper, darker to begin surfacing over time? Perhaps the realization that something was off started subtly, a twisting of your words, a creeping doubt in your own memory, a gnawing feeling that something just wasn't right you couldn't quite place. Yet, by the time you truly question what is happening, you may have already been tangled in a web of manipulation.

These aren't just uncomfortable encounters. They're calculated patterns—strategies individuals use, often with antisocial traits, to influence, dominate, and erode the autonomy of those around them. What feels like confusion or chaos to the victim is, for the manipulator, a carefully orchestrated game.

In this chapter, we will explore various methods used by those with antisocial personalities to exert influence over others. By recognizing these patterns, we aim to provide insights into how manipulators operate, equipping you with an understanding that will help build resilience against being pulled into their dark game.

Methods to Gain Control

To understand the mindset of an antisocial manipulator, one must first recognize the deliberate and calculated ways in which they establish control. These individuals are not guided by empathy or mutual respect but rather by the drive to dominate and influence others to serve their own ends. The methods they use are often subtle at first, woven into interactions that may seem ordinary or even affectionate. Yet beneath the surface lies a strategic intent—to undermine autonomy, exploit vulnerabilities, and slowly erode the victim's sense of agency. By examining the most common methods of control, we can begin to dismantle the illusion of trust these individuals create and recognize the red flags before the grip tightens.

Coercive Techniques

Coercion ranks among the most powerful tools in a manipulator's arsenal. Those with antisocial tendencies often use intimidation—whether through subtle suggestions or overt threats—to gain swift and often unquestioned control. These tactics rely on instilling fear or anxiety and pressuring victims into compliance.

The psychological toll can be gradual but drastic: victims may start out walking on eggshells, feel trapped, and be dependent on the manipulator as a means of avoiding conflict or harm. For instance, in a romantic relationship, one partner might insist that the other cut ties with friends or family, threatening to withdraw financial support if they refuse.

Recognizing coercion begins with identifying its common patterns—threats to physical safety, emotional security, or financial stability.

Baiting and Hooking

Manipulators don't always lead with fear—sometimes, they begin with charm and later use your connection as leverage. Baiting and hooking is a tactic rooted in flattery, attention, and affection, creating a rush of euphoria that disarms the victim. For example, a charming coworker might shower praise on you for your contributions, frequently offering to take you out for coffee or lunch, all while subtly steering conversations to learn about your doubts and weaknesses, to later use against you.

Those aware of this tactic understand that the manipulator's affection often comes with strings attached—expectations, subtle control, or emotional dependence. Maintaining vigilance in the face of intense praise or an unnaturally quick attempt to bond is essential. The ability to enjoy connection while staying grounded in reality can keep individuals from becoming entangled in harmful dynamics cloaked in charisma.

Isolation Tactics

Another deeply destabilizing strategy is isolation, where manipulators work to weaken or sever ties between the victim and their support network. By doing so, they leave their victim increasingly reliant on their companionship and support, diminishing their autonomy.

This tactic often involves creating conflicts with friends or family, spreading false rumors, or planting seeds of doubt that loved ones have the victim's best interest in mind. For example, a jealous partner might insist that their significant other stop seeing friends or family, claiming that these relationships are toxic or that they don't truly care about them.

Isolation can lead to a sense of loneliness and helplessness, as victims of isolation tactics end up cut off from those who might offer the support or perspective to help them recognize or deflect manipulation.

Feigning Victimhood

Another particularly insidious method employed by manipulators is feigning victimhood. Here, the manipulator seeks to exploit the natural human tendency to sympathize with those who appear to be suffering or in distress. By presenting themselves as the wronged party, manipulators can divert attention away from their own behavior and instead position themselves as those in need of rescue or support.

Identifying this tactic demands skepticism and an ability to assess situations objectively, asking whether the purported victim consistently demonstrates such patterns or if this is an anomaly meant to obscure their behavior. By learning to discern genuine grievances from manipulation, individuals can remain aware of any attempts to control or exploit their sympathies.

These tactics, though distinct, are often interconnected and combined in ways that have an insidious impact on their victims' ability to discern and identify them. Each strategy is designed to render the victim increasingly pliable and reliant on the manipulator, stripping away autonomy and self-confidence. By understanding not only the individual tactics but also the overarching goal of such manipulation, individuals can take decisive steps to protect themselves. Education provides empowerment, allowing potential victims to anticipate manipulative strategies as they arise and take preemptive measures.

Psychological Manipulation Techniques

After establishing dominance, antisocial individuals typically employ a range of additional psychological manipulation techniques to manipulate, control, and exploit their targets. These tactics are not random. They are calculated tools designed to erode self-trust, isolate support systems, and create psychological dependency. What may at first seem like confusion or miscommunication often reveals itself as a deliberate strategy.

Narcissistic Projection

Narcissistic projection is a psychological sleight-of-hand in which a manipulator attributes their own undesirable traits, emotions, or intentions to someone else. It's a defense mechanism turned weapon—used not just to avoid self-reflection but to confuse and destabilize the target. This tactic functions as a diversion, redirecting attention away from the manipulator's flaws and placing the other person on the defensive.

For example, a partner might accuse the other of being selfish or uncaring precisely when that person is asserting a basic emotional or physical need. In doing so, the manipulator is able to avoid accountability while simultaneously undermining the target's confidence in their own need or value. Over time, this can lead to self-doubt and confusion, especially if the target begins to internalize the projected traits.

Manipulative Flattery

Manipulative flattery, unlike direct emotional manipulation, operates under the guise of admiration. Entering through seemingly innocuous comments like, "You're the only one who truly understands me," this tactic cloaks the manipulator's intentions in a veil of praise. Predators use such flattery to erode defenses, making the target comfortable with over-disclosure, which can later be used to exploit vulnerabilities.

What makes manipulative flattery particularly deceptive is that it can feel incredibly validating, especially to those who are emotionally open or eager for connection. But the praise is often calculated, aimed not at celebrating the other person but at softening them for eventual control. Over time, this seemingly affectionate behavior can erode boundaries and make the target more pliable to influence.

Gaslighting

Gaslighting stands out as one of the most insidious forms of psychological manipulation because it directly attacks and revises a person's sense of reality. At its core, gaslighting is about making someone doubt their own perceptions and memories and often rewriting their entire perspective. It subtly undermines trust in oneself, leading victims to question their judgments and experiences.

The term 'gaslighting' originates from the play *Gas Light*, in which a husband manipulates his wife into believing she's going insane by dimming the lights in their home and denying it's happening, distorting her ability to trust her own experience.

Many victims describe a growing sense of insecurity accompanied by gnawing self-doubt. They might withdraw socially, hesitant to engage in conversations where their opinions might be undermined again. This distortion of self-trust can lead to anxiety and depression. Being constantly told your reality is flawed leaves individuals walking on metaphorical eggshells, overly cautious to avoid further manipulation. Over time, this can erode self-esteem.

Guilt and Shame

Antisocial individuals often use guilt or shame as tools to undermine self-worth and steer behavior. Guilt might surface in statements like, "After all I've done for you, how could you refuse me?" This manipulative twist makes the target responsible for the manipulator's emotions, thus ensuring compliance.

Similarly, shame can manifest in comments such as, "I can't believe you would choose them over me; you're so ungrateful," instilling a feeling of unworthiness and inadequacy in the target. This strategy further weakens the target's self-esteem and sense of agency. The target, primed to avoid the discomfort of both guilt and shame, is likely to act according to the manipulator's desires to alleviate these negative emotions. Recognizing these guilt and shame tactics can empower one to establish emotional boundaries and reduce susceptibility to manipulation.

These psychological manipulation techniques typically aren't standalone tactics; they intertwine, compounding their impact. Emotional exploitation often forms the bedrock for other manipulations. Guilt and shame weaken defenses, enabling false narratives and manipulative flattery to pull targets deep into the web of control. Once an individual is ensnared, narcissistic projection comfortably resides in their weakened self-conception, reshaping self-perception to mirror whatever the manipulator desires.

Understanding these techniques allows individuals to equip themselves with strategies to counteract their effects. Spotting guilt-inducing scenarios, identifying praise-masking manipulation, recognizing distorted stories, and discerning projected attributes are vital for preserving autonomy. Cultivating awareness of these tactics encourages individuals to maintain emotional distance and prevents manipulators from easily infiltrating their psyche.

Case Study: The Covert Manipulator

To outsiders, Marcus was magnetic—quick-witted, attentive, and effortlessly likable. He could speak at length about art, politics, or quantum theory with equal ease. Within months of meeting him, Sarah, a graphic designer in her early 30s, found herself swept into what felt like a whirlwind romance. He brought flowers to her office, cooked elaborate dinners, and peppered her world with affection and praise. It felt like destiny.

But beneath the surface of his charm, Marcus harbored a dark personality—one consistent with antisocial personality disorder (ASPD), characterized by a persistent disregard for others' rights, manipulation, and a lack of empathy or remorse.

The shift in their relationship was subtle at first. A sarcastic comment dressed as a joke. A raised eyebrow made her second-guess her memory. A lingering silence followed after she expressed an opinion. Over time, Sarah found herself apologizing more often, unsure of what she'd done wrong. Marcus rarely raised his voice. His cruelty was administered in whispers and smirks, in forgotten birthdays and sudden withdrawal of affection.

Psychological control, especially when rooted in ASPD, rarely erupts in violence. It seeps in through gaslighting, triangulation, and calculated emotional starvation. Marcus would isolate Sarah gradually, expressing vague concerns about her friends—how "needy" they were, how they "used her." He positioned himself as her sole confidant, the only one who "truly understood" her. When she tried to set boundaries, he'd accuse her of being selfish or unstable, often referencing incidents that never happened to undermine her sense of reality.

This is the hallmark of the covert manipulator—a predator who doesn't need to raise a fist because they've already taken control of the mind. After speaking to her therapist about her concerns, Sarah began keeping journals to track events, noticing discrepancies between what she experienced and what Marcus claimed had occurred.

Marcus, like many with ASPD, exhibited instrumental empathy, the ability to read emotions not for connection but for leverage. He knew what to say to get forgiveness, how to cry at the right moment, and when to show vulnerability to draw her back in. Each time Sarah tried to leave, he would become the perfect partner again, until she stayed, and the cycle resumed. Sarah had been subjected to prolonged emotional abuse that had been hidden and insidious. Ultimately, it was the pattern itself that became her wake-up call. The consistency of the rise and fall, the sweet and the sour, the patterns that no longer seemed random.

Cold and Calculated

Control is rarely seized all at once. More often, it is given away—bit by bit—under the influence of charm, confusion, and calculated manipulation. As we've seen, individuals with antisocial traits often rely not on brute force but on psychological tactics that disorient, isolate, and dominate. Their power lies in their subtlety, their ability to make others doubt themselves while appearing blameless.

Understanding these strategies is the first step in breaking free from them. Recognizing the larger patterns of manipulation like gaslighting, love bombing, and emotional withdrawal allows us to name what was once invisible—and in doing so, reclaim our sense of agency. But insight alone is not enough. In the next chapter, we'll shift from analysis to action. You'll learn what to do when to spot red flags of dangerous behavior, how to set firm boundaries, and how to safeguard your well-being when confronted with antisocial personalities.

Chapter 8:

Protecting Yourself—Practical Strategies Against Antisocial Personalities

Have you ever felt like someone else was quietly pulling the strings—subtly influencing your choices, shaping your reactions—while you struggled to reclaim a sense of control? Recognizing manipulation is a first step towards personal safety, but full protection lies in knowing how to act in the best way in the face of these encounters.

In this chapter, we'll explore how to respond calmly and effectively when faced with individuals who exhibit warning signs of manipulation or danger. You'll also learn how to strengthen your internal compass through self-awareness, confidence, and intuition. We'll also explore practical tools, such as legal protections, support networks, and therapeutic approaches that can help you regain your footing during and after encounters with antisocial personalities. By understanding these strategies, you'll be better equipped to navigate harmful dynamics, protect your autonomy, and even support others facing similar challenges.

Response Strategies to Dangerous Individuals

When faced with someone who exhibits manipulative or predatory behavior, remember this above all else—you owe no one your time, explanation, or emotional openness, especially when something feels off. Antisocial individuals often rely on a mix of charm and pressure, exploiting your empathy and discomfort to break down your boundaries.

Your intuition is a powerful internal alarm system that is too often dismissed. If someone gives you a strange feeling—whether through subtle intimidation, pushy behavior, or excessive charm—trust that signal. You don't need hard proof to step back or disengage. Feeling uneasy is enough.

Create Distance Early

When something doesn't feel right, create space—physically, emotionally, or digitally. That might mean excusing yourself from a conversation, crossing the street, deleting a message, or simply declining an invitation. Manipulative people often test boundaries by ignoring social cues or pressuring you to stay engaged. Be calm and firm: "I need to go now," or "I'm not interested, thanks." You don't owe further explanation.

Context is your ally. Awareness of your surroundings can help you assess whether a situation poses a risk. Consider the time of day, the setting, and the presence and demeanor of others nearby. A bustling café mid-morning is not the same as a dim alley at night. These elements shape the safest course of action—whether it's wiser to speak plainly or to remove yourself quietly. Watch for subtle cues: a shift in tone, sudden silence, avoidance of eye contact, or fidgeting. These signs can signal an escalation or discomfort, nudging you to act quickly and re-establish distance.

Set Clear Boundaries

Establishing boundaries serves as a protective mechanism, both mentally and physically. Clearly stating what is and isn't acceptable can interrupt a manipulator's momentum. The clarity of your words and steady posture form a barrier that communicates strength and resolve.

If someone persists in crossing your boundaries—invading your space, talking over you, or refusing to back off—respond with calm directness: "Please respect my space." Step back if needed. The key is to state your limits without explaining them. Dangerous individuals often feed on emotional responses, using them to manipulate or provoke.

Stick to short, firm responses: "No." "That doesn't work for me." "I've already said no." Repetition reinforces your stance and shows you won't be swayed by pressure or guilt.

Project Calm Confidence

Because antisocial individuals often look for vulnerable targets, your overall demeanor has the power to change the course of the situation. Simple techniques, like maintaining a calm tone and deliberate breathing, can help diffuse potential threats or de-escalate a dynamic that could have become dangerous.

Additionally, projecting an aura of self-assurance and awareness can deter aggressors, signaling that you are not an easy target. Cultivating these skills not only enhances personal safety but also empowers individuals to navigate challenging social interactions with confidence.

Build and Lean on Support Systems

Support systems are vital, both for validation and protection. Creating a robust network of trusted individuals—friends, family, or professional allies—ensures you have a lifeline in distressing situations. Sharing personal encounters with them offers perspective and fortifies awareness. This communal safety net not only helps in preemptive measures but also aids in post-incident recovery, providing emotional support and practical assistance.

At work or in shared living spaces, reporting manipulative or concerning behavior—even before it becomes overtly dangerous—can help create accountability and build a record. You're not overreacting; you're exercising foresight. In more serious situations, don't hesitate to involve authorities. Timely reporting may prevent further harm, not just to you but to others as well.

These strategies lay the groundwork for personal safety and emotional resilience in the face of harmful individuals. Recognizing response strategies empowers you with the clarity and control essential in maintaining composure amid life's uncertainties. It arms you with preventative measures and imbues a sense of agency, which is foundational in cultivating mental fortitude.

Building Personal Resilience

True resilience begins from within. When faced with manipulative or harmful individuals, your greatest defense isn't just strategic; it's the quiet strength of self-trust and inner confidence, both of which allow you to heed your intuition and set boundaries in a way that provides inherent protection from predatory individuals.

Know Your Triggers

Creating internal confidence starts with self-awareness. When you understand your emotional triggers, you stop being surprised by them. Instead of reacting impulsively, you recognize what's happening inside you and can respond with clarity. Perhaps you notice a tendency to people-please or feel thrown off by praise followed by pressure. By naming these patterns, you reclaim control over your responses.

Stay Grounded

Mindfulness supports this process by anchoring you in the present. Simple techniques—like pausing to take three deep breaths, or doing a grounding practice such as the 5-4-3-2-1 method—help shift you out of anxiety and into awareness. The more often you return to yourself in moments of stress, the more natural it becomes to stay centered even when someone is trying to manipulate or provoke you.

Critical Thinking

Critical thinking as a habit is another key to inner strength. When someone's behavior feels off or you have a feeling you can't quite explain, get curious. Ask yourself of the person you have just encountered: *What might they gain from this? Is this consistent with how trustworthy people behave? How well do I know this person?* Confidence grows not from knowing all the answers but from trusting your ability to ask the right questions and wait for clarity to emerge.

Tune Into Emotion

Emotional intelligence deepens this resilience. It helps you recognize when others are acting from insecurity, fear, or control—so you don't absorb their energy as your own. When someone downplays your voice or pushes your boundaries, emotional intelligence lets you notice their tactics without taking them personally. You stop seeing their behavior as a reflection of your worth and start seeing it as information.

Resilience isn't about becoming invulnerable. It's about knowing that whatever arises—manipulation, discomfort, uncertainty—you can meet it with self-awareness and grace. The more you strengthen that relationship with yourself, the less power external pressure has over you.

Legal Resources

Personal resilience and self-awareness are essential precursors to legal protection. Recognizing when manipulation crosses into abuse allows you to turn inward insight into outward action. Understanding your rights transforms confusion and fear into empowered decision-making.

Documentation as a Legal Tool

If you're facing manipulation—especially in the workplace or in personal relationships—document everything: record dates, times, specific behaviors, and any communication. This transforms emotional experiences into concrete evidence, supporting potential legal claims and offering clarity should you pursue action.

Understanding Restraining Orders

Restraining orders are more than symbolic; they create legal boundaries against harassment or abuse. A temporary order offers immediate protection and can later be extended through a formal court process. Learning how to file for one in your location should you ever need to removes the fear of the unknown and places safety within reach.

The process of obtaining a restraining order can empower individuals by affirming their rights and addressing their concerns regarding personal safety. It serves as a critical tool for those feeling vulnerable, allowing them to reclaim a sense of agency in the face of intimidation or violence.

Additionally, understanding the related resources available—such as legal assistance or support networks—can provide invaluable guidance, ensuring that individuals are not alone in their journey to seek protection and justice.

Know Your Rights and Resources

Getting acquainted with legal aid is an empowering step. Many believe legal support is financially out of reach, but numerous resources exist to bridge this gap. Non-profit organizations, university legal clinics, and government-funded programs often offer pro bono or sliding scale services. These resources ensure that financial constraints don't hinder access to justice. A dedicated legal professional helps navigate the complexities of your situation, offering advice tailored to protect your rights and safety.

In addition to knowing what legal support you have available, there is a great deal of value in knowing your rights related to challenging situations as they arise. Whether it's employment laws protecting against workplace bullying or tenant rights safeguarding against a landlord violating your privacy, understanding these protections can preemptively neutralize manipulative tactics.

Knowledge of privacy laws, for instance, equips you to challenge unauthorized surveillance or breaches of personal data. Awareness of whistleblower protections can encourage individuals to report unethical behavior in organizations or communities without the fear of retribution. Each legal right you gain information on serves as an invisible yet powerful barrier dissuading would-be manipulators.

While the legal system is a formidable ally, it's equally important to recognize its limitations. Legal measures are primarily about protection and deterrence; they seldom address the emotional aftermath of manipulation and abuse. This brings us to our next point—therapeutic support. Emotional healing is as vital as legal protection when it comes to addressing what leaves us vulnerable to dangerous individuals.

Therapeutic Interventions

While legal support helps protect your rights, therapy addresses something equally vital—understanding why you may have been vulnerable to manipulation in the first place. Beneath the surface of any harmful dynamic often lies a tangle of unmet needs, old wounds, and unconscious patterns. Therapy offers the space to gently unpack these, transforming pain into insight and insight into resilience.

Therapy may offer the space to explore the personal history that shaped your emotional responses. Why did you overlook the red flags? What made you second-guess your instincts or prioritize someone else's comfort over your safety? These aren't questions of blame—they're paths to clarity. Modalities like trauma-informed therapy and inner child work can help reveal the root of longstanding beliefs that may have left you susceptible to harmful relationships or environments.

Rewriting Internal Narratives to Build Confidence

Manipulation often feeds on internal narratives of unworthiness, guilt, or fear. In therapy, you learn to challenge and reframe these stories. Cognitive behavioral therapy (CBT) is especially useful in disrupting patterns of self-doubt and replacing them with thoughts rooted in self-trust and clarity. As you examine the beliefs that kept you stuck, you begin to replace them with ones that support your strength and sovereignty.

As therapy helps you make sense of past dynamics, it also equips you to protect yourself in the future. You'll gain tools for setting healthy boundaries, recognizing early signs of manipulation, and speaking up without fear. This growing self-assurance becomes a kind of quiet armor—an inner confidence that subtly deters those who prey on insecurity. When you radiate clarity and self-respect, it becomes harder for manipulators to find a foothold.

To do this work effectively, finding a therapist who understands trauma and relational abuse is key. Seek someone experienced in helping clients unravel manipulation and rebuild personal agency. Whether through professional directories, word-of-mouth recommendations, or online support communities, the right therapist becomes a co-architect in your healing—guiding, not directing, your process.

Ultimately, therapy isn't just about recovering from manipulation—it's about becoming someone who no longer attracts or tolerates it. You emerge with a deeper understanding of yourself, a stronger sense of what you deserve, and the ability to walk away from anything that doesn't align. The process of healing becomes a process of becoming someone confident, self-aware, and whole.

Case Study: Escape From the Charm

Sam's story begins like many others—charmed by a seemingly perfect partner. At first, his relationship with Olivia felt like a whirlwind of affection, attention, and validation. She was everything Sam thought he needed, offering a constant stream of compliments, plans for the future, and a sense of belonging he hadn't felt in years. But beneath this facade, a far darker reality was taking shape. Sam soon realized that Olivia's charm wasn't just a trait—it was a tool.

The first signs were subtle. Olivia would make small, offhand comments about Sam's friends, family, and even his career choices—nothing overtly offensive, but just enough to sow seeds of doubt. At first, Sam brushed it off, thinking it was harmless. As time passed, however, the manipulation deepened. Olivia began to isolate Sam from his social circle, casting doubt on their loyalty and intentions. His once-supportive friendships began to crumble, replaced by Olivia's need for constant reassurance and control.

The real turning point came one evening when Sam found himself questioning his own memory. Olivia would twist past conversations and events to paint him as unreasonable or overly sensitive. At first, Sam was convinced that he was the one misremembering things. But with every instance, the doubt grew—was he really the problem, or was Olivia manipulating the narrative?

Sam's breakthrough didn't come from a single moment of clarity. It was the slow accumulation of feelings: confusion, self-doubt, and the increasing realization that he felt like a shell of his former self. The more Sam analyzed his relationship, the more he saw how deeply embedded manipulation was. Olivia's ability to charm, disarm, and then undermine him was a deliberate pattern—a strategy of control veiled in sweetness and attention.

But it wasn't until Sam started therapy that the pieces truly began to fall into place. At first, he was unsure how therapy could help with what he thought were just relationship issues. However, as he worked through his feelings with his therapist, he began to uncover the deep psychological toll manipulation had taken on him over the years. His therapist helped him understand the emotional hooks that had been set by Olivia—how his vulnerabilities had been exploited and why he hadn't seen it sooner.

Through therapy, Sam learned about antisocial personalities, gaslighting, and coercive control. This newfound knowledge was revolutionary. He realized that Olivia's behavior was not a series of isolated incidents but part of a carefully crafted pattern designed to destabilize him. As Sam learned more about these tactics, his ability to recognize them in real time grew stronger. With therapeutic insights and guidance, Sam began to reclaim his autonomy.

The process of leaving wasn't easy. Olivia's charm made every goodbye feel like an impossibility, but Sam had learned to trust his newfound understanding of manipulation. He could no longer ignore the red flags that had once felt like minor inconveniences. Armed with his therapist's support, Sam started to set boundaries. He stopped engaging in the endless cycles of argument and apology that had been the cornerstone of their dynamic.

Eventually, Sam made the decision to end the relationship. It was a difficult and painful step, but it was also empowering. For the first time in months, he felt like he was in control of his life again. Therapy had given him not just the tools to exit but the clarity to understand why he had been vulnerable to such a relationship in the first place.

In the months that followed, Sam worked on rebuilding his life and healing from the emotional scars left by the relationship. With his therapist's guidance, he gained confidence in his ability to spot manipulation and safeguard his boundaries. What had once been an overwhelming burden now became a source of strength, and Sam emerged from the experience more resilient than he ever thought possible.

Sam's journey shows that the process of recognizing manipulation is not just about escaping—it's about understanding why it happened in the first place. Through therapy, Sam not only learned to leave the relationship but also to reclaim his autonomy, confidence, and sense of self. His rise to resilience became not just an escape from harm but a reclamation of his own power, leaving him prepared to face future challenges with clarity and strength.

Empowerment and Awareness

Knowing how to respond in tricky situations, setting firm boundaries, and building a reliable support system are key steps in defending yourself against manipulation. The tools we have explored—such as de-escalation techniques and sharp critical thinking—do not just protect you from the chilling psychopaths you might cross paths with; they also strengthen your mental resilience for encounters with subtly harmful individuals who are likely to try to manipulate and control you in everyday life, from your workplace to your community.

This journey is about more than just surviving difficult situations; it's about growing stronger and more aware. The more you understand, the more confident you become in facing manipulative behaviors without letting them shake you. Ultimately, given the prevalence of antisocial individuals in our society, arming yourself with these skills and insights could ensure you know how to manage both overt and covert threats and could even save your life.

Conclusion

When considering how to protect ourselves against antisocial personalities, sociopaths, and psychopaths, it is useful to reflect on the complexity of these individuals and the far-reaching impact they can have on others. These are not merely one-dimensional villains from a storybook but often charismatic, manipulative, and highly skilled at concealing their intentions. Gaining insight into the minds of those who deceive, exploit, and harm—and understanding the psychological, environmental, and neurological factors that contribute to the development of the criminal or antisocial mind—can be both eye-opening and deeply empowering.

By learning how to recognize these individuals, we begin to reclaim something precious: our power, our sense of safety, and our confidence in our own perceptions.

In that sense, this book was never simply about understanding the minds of the dangerous few who walk among us; it was meant to empower you, the reader, with the tools to recognize, respond to, and protect yourself from the damaging effects of manipulation and abuse so that you might have more freedom and genuine connection in your life.

While most of us will thankfully never cross paths with a serial killer or a profoundly dangerous predator, manipulation comes in many forms. It can wear a friendly face or disguise itself as love, loyalty, or guidance. Yet even these "lesser" forms of harm—chronic gaslighting, emotional coercion, boundary violations—can leave deep imprints. The slow erosion of trust, the isolation from support systems, and the creeping doubt in your own judgment can cause pain that lingers long after the individual is gone. These effects are often invisible to others, but they are no less real and no less damaging.

While understanding the psychology of antisocial individuals is critical, the true power lies in knowing your own mind. You can achieve greater personal security by strengthening your emotional resilience, trust in your intuition, and confidence to set calm, firm boundaries.

For those of us who are recovering from a harmful encounter, resilience is not merely about surviving the encounter with a sociopath or psychopath; it is about learning and growing from the experience so that we are protected in the future. It is about recognizing that, while you may have been vulnerable at one point in time, you now possess the tools to identify those same red flags in the future. You are no longer a passive participant in life's sometimes painful lessons; you are an active agent of your own healing and safety.

In closing, I encourage you to move forward with this newfound awareness in hand. While it can be frightening to realize how common dangerous individuals are, we don't need to let it impact our ability to experience and enjoy our lives deeply. Don't live in fear; instead, walk confidently, knowing that in your future encounters—whether personal or professional—you carry the power of knowledge.

While vigilance is always recommended, you can also find confidence in the recognition that you are now far less susceptible to the lies, manipulations, and harm of others. You are equipped to protect your heart and mind, not just from those who would physically hurt you but from anyone or anything that seeks to diminish your sense of self through coercion or abuse. Allow this clarity to serve as a beacon that will guide you, even through storms of uncertainty, illuminating a clear path for your truest self, secure in the knowledge that you can keep yourself safe.

References

Aharoni, E., Abdulla, S., Allen, C. H., & Nadelhoffer, T. (2022). Ethical implications of neurobiologically informed risk assessment for criminal justice decisions: A case for pragmatism. In F. De Brigard & W. Sinnott-Armstrong (Eds.), *Neuroscience and philosophy* (pp. xx–xx). MIT Press. https://www.ncbi.nlm.nih.gov/books/NBK583716/

Alegria, A. A., Blanco, C., Petry, N. M., Skodol, A. E., Liu, S.-M., Grant, B., & Hasin, D. (2013). Sex differences in antisocial personality disorder. *Personality Disorders: Theory, Research, and Treatment, 4*(3), 214–222. https://doi.org/10.1037/a0031681

American Psychiatric Association. (2013). *Diagnostic and Statistical Manual of Mental Disorders* (5th ed.). American Psychiatric Publishing.

Anderson, N. E., & Kiehl, K. A. (2014). Psychopathy: Developmental perspectives. *Restorative Neurology and Neuroscience, 32*(1), 103–117. https://doi.org/10.3233/RNN-139001

Antisocial Personality Disorder: Symptoms & treatment. (2017, March 10). Cleveland Clinic. https://my.clevelandclinic.org/health/diseases/9657-antisocial-personality-disorder

Balsis, S., Woods, C. M., Gleason, M. E. J., & Oltmanns, T. F. (2007). Overdiagnosis and Underdiagnosis of Personality Disorders in Older Adults. *The American Journal of Geriatric Psychiatry, 15*(9), 742–753. https://doi.org/10.1097/jgp.0b013e31813c6b4e

Bezdjian, S., Baker, L. A., & Tuvblad, C. (2011). Genetic and environmental influences on impulsivity: A meta-analysis of twin, family and adoption studies. *Clinical Psychology Review, 31*(7), 1209–1223. https://doi.org/10.1016/j.cpr.2011.07.005

Bjørnebekk, G. (2021). Possible interventions for preventing the development of psychopathic traits among children and adolescents? *International Journal of Environmental Research and Public Health*, *19*(1), 409. https://doi.org/10.3390/ijerph19010409

Black, D. (2015, July). *The natural history of Antisocial Personality Disorder.* ResearchGate. https://www.researchgate.net/publication/280123062_The_Natural_History_of_Antisocial_Personality_Disorder

Bonn, S. (2014). *The sociopath-serial killer connection.* Psychology Today. https://www.psychologytoday.com/us/blog/wicked-deeds/201409/the-sociopath-serial-killer-connection

Buckholtz, J. W., Treadway, M. T., Cowan, R. L., Woodward, N. D., Benning, S. D., Li, R., Ansari, M. S., Baldwin, R. M., Schwartzman, A. N., Shelby, E. S., Smith, C. E., Cole, D., Kessler, R. M., & Zald, D. H. (2010). Mesolimbic dopamine reward system hypersensitivity in individuals with psychopathic traits. *Nature Neuroscience*, *13*(4), 419–421. https://doi.org/10.1038/nn.2510

Carr, N. (2024, August 14). *How to treat antisocial personality disorder.* MentalHealth.com. https://www.mentalhealth.com/library/treating-antisocial-personality-disorder

Cleckley, H. M. (1941). *The mask of sanity: An attempt to reinterpret the so-called psychopathic personality.* The C.V. Mosby Company.

Cope, L. M., Shane, M. S., Segall, J. M., Nyalakanti, P. K., Stevens, M. C., Pearlson, G. D., Calhoun, V. D., & Kiehl, K. A. (2012). Examining the effect of psychopathic traits on gray matter volume in a community substance abuse sample. *Psychiatry Research: Neuroimaging*, *204*(2-3), 91–100. https://doi.org/10.1016/j.pscychresns.2012.10.004

Corbit, L., Kendig, M., & Moul, C. (2019). The role of serotonin 1B in the representation of outcomes. *Scientific Reports, 9*(1), Article 38938. https://doi.org/10.1038/s41598-019-38938-4

Cruz, D., Lichten, M., Berg, K., & George, P. (2022). Developmental trauma: Conceptual framework, associated risks and comorbidities, and evaluation and treatment. *Frontiers in Psychiatry*, *13*(1), 1–14. https://doi.org/10.3389/fpsyt.2022.800687

DeAngelis, T. (2022, March 1). *A broader view of psychopathy*. American Psychological Association. https://www.apa.org/monitor/2022/03/ce-corner-psychopathy

First, M. B., Bender, D. S., Oldham, J. M., & Skodol, A. E. (2018). *User's guide for the SCID-5-AMPD: Structured clinical interview for the DSM-5 alternative model for personality disorders.* American Psychiatric Association Publishing.

Fisher, K. A., Hany, M., & Torrico, T. J. (2024, February 29). *Antisocial Personality Disorder.* National Library of Medicine; StatPearls Publishing. https://www.ncbi.nlm.nih.gov/books/NBK546673/

Flaaten, E., Langfeldt, M., & Morken, K. (2024). Antisocial personality disorder and therapeutic pessimism – how can mentalization-based treatment contribute to an increased therapeutic optimism among health professionals? *Frontiers in Psychology*, *15*(1). https://doi.org/10.3389/fpsyg.2024.1320405

Floyd, A. E., & Gupta, V. (2023). *Minnesota multiphasic personality inventory*. PubMed; StatPearls Publishing. https://www.ncbi.nlm.nih.gov/books/NBK557525/

Johanson, M., Vaurio, O., Tiihonen, J., & Lähteenvuo, M. (2020). A systematic literature review of neuroimaging of psychopathic traits. *Frontiers in Psychiatry*, *10*(1027). https://doi.org/10.3389/fpsyt.2019.01027

Jones, D. N., & Paulhus, D. L. (2017). Duplicity among the dark triad: Three faces of deceit. *Journal of Personality and Social Psychology, 113*(2), 329–342. https://doi.org/10.1037/pspp0000139

Kaufman, J. (2010). Nature, nurture, and the development and prevention of antisocial behavior problems in children. *Journal of the American Academy of Child and Adolescent Psychiatry*, *49*(4), 300. https://pmc.ncbi.nlm.nih.gov/articles/PMC3750495/

Kaylor, L. (1999). Antisocial Personality Disorder: Diagnostic, ethical and treatment issues. *Issues in Mental Health Nursing*, *20*(3), 247–258. https://doi.org/10.1080/016128499248646

Koenigs, M. (2012). The role of prefrontal cortex in psychopathy. *Reviews in the Neurosciences*, *23*(3). https://doi.org/10.1515/revneuro-2012-0036

Haghighi, A. S. (2021, July 6). Psychopath vs. sociopath: How do they differ? *Medical News Today*.https://www.medicalnewstoday.com/articles/psychopath-vs-sociopath#summary

Hunter, P. (2010). The psycho gene. *EMBO Reports*, *11*(9), 667–669. https://doi.org/10.1038/embor.2010.122

Liubov, R. (2013). Family influence on formation of children's manipulative attitudes. *International Journal of Cognitive Research in Science, Engineering and Education, 1*(1).https://www.researchgate.net/publication/313366572_Family_influence_on_formation_of_children

McLean, S. (2018). *Emotional dysregulation in children who have experienced adversity.* Australian Institute of Family Studies. https://aifs.gov.au/resources/practice-guides/developmental-differences-children-who-have-experienced-adversity-guide-no1

Martens, W. H. J. (2008). The problem with Robert Hare's psychopathy checklist: Incorrect conclusions, high risk of misuse, and lack of reliability. *Medicine and Law*, *27*(2), 449–462.

https://www.researchgate.net/publication/23162155_The_problem_with_Robert_Hare

Moeller, F. G., & Dougherty, D. M. (2024). Antisocial Personality Disorder, alcohol, and aggression. *Alcohol Research & Health, 25*(1), 5. https://pmc.ncbi.nlm.nih.gov/articles/PMC6707114/

Mulder, R. T. (2012). Cultural aspects of personality disorder. *The Oxford Handbook of Personality Disorders*, 259–274. https://doi.org/10.1093/oxfordhb/9780199735013.013.0013

Ozarin, L. (2001). Moral insanity: A brief history. *Psychiatric News, 36*(10), 21–21. https://doi.org/10.1176/pn.36.10.0021

Pickersgill, M. (2011). Standardising antisocial personality disorder: The social shaping of a psychiatric technology. *Sociology of Health & Illness, 34*(4), 544–559. https://doi.org/10.1111/j.1467-9566.2011.01404.x

Plackett, B. (2021, August 8). The neurological differences between psychopaths and sociopaths. *Discover Magazine*.https://www.discovermagazine.com/mind/the-neurological-differences-between-psychopaths-and-sociopaths

Salekin, R. T., Rogers, R., & Sewell, K. W. (1996). A review and meta-analysis of the Psychopathy Checklist and Psychopathy Checklist—Revised: Predictive validity of dangerousness. *Clinical Psychology: Science and Practice, 3*(3), 203–215. https://doi.org/10.1111/j.1468-2850.1996.tb00071.x

Segal, N. L. (1995). Pathways to sociopathy: Twin analyses offer direction. *Behavioral and Brain Sciences, 18*(3), 574–575. https://doi.org/10.1017/s0140525x00039960

Seid, M., Anbesaw, T., Melke, S., Beteshe, D., Mussa, H., Asmamaw, A., & Shegaw, M. (2022). Antisocial personality disorder and associated factors among incarcerated in prison. *BMC Psychiatry, 22*(1). https://doi.org/10.1186/s12888-022-03710-y

Silverio, S. A., Lyons, M. T., & Burton, S. P. (2023). Dangerously intelligent: A call for re-evaluating psychopathy using perceptions of intelligence. *Journal of Intelligence, 11*(2), 25. https://doi.org/10.3390/jintelligence11020025

Silvers, A. (2024, December 7). How to spot a sociopathic liar. *Ann Silvers, MA.* https://annsilvers.com/blogs/news/how-sociopaths-fool-you-with-their-lies

Tuvblad, C., & Beaver, K. M. (2013). Genetic and environmental influences on antisocial behavior. *Journal of Criminal Justice, 41*(5), 273–276. https://doi.org/10.1016/j.jcrimjus.2013.07.007

Whitfield-Gabrieli, S., & Ford, J. M. (2012). Default Mode Network activity and connectivity in psychopathology. *Annual Review of Clinical Psychology, 8*(1), 49–76. https://doi.org/10.1146/annurev-clinpsy-032511-143049

Williams, N. (2023, May 9). Effects of antisocial personality disorder in relationships. *Marriage.com.*https://www.marriage.com/advice/mental-health/aspd-in-relationships/

Yang, Y., Raine, A., Narr, K. L., Colletti, P., & Toga, A. W. (2009). Localization of deformations within the amygdala in individuals with psychopathy. *Archives of General Psychiatry, 66*(9), 986. https://doi.org/10.1001/archgenpsychiatry.2009.110

Image References

Bolovtsova, E. (2021, February 16). *Couple looking at each other* [Image]. Pexels. https://www.pexels.com/photo/couple-looking-at-each-other-6474944/

Chuck, W. (2020, October 20). *Side view of a good-looking man with facial hair* [Image]. Pexels. https://www.pexels.com/photo/side-view-of-a-good-looking-man-with-facial-hair-5534410/

Constance, K. (2024, March 3). *Man smoking cigarette* [Image]. Pexels. https://www.pexels.com/photo/man-smoking-cigarette-18424591/

Cottonbro studio. (2020, January 29). *Couple having a misunderstanding* [Image]. Pexels. https://www.pexels.com/photo/couple-having-a-misunderstanding-3692885/

Cottonbro studio. (2020, October 13). *Crying woman with flowing mascara on sad face* [Image]. Pexels. https://www.pexels.com/photo/crying-woman-with-flowing-mascara-on-sad-face-5537877/

Cottonbro studio. (2021, November 11). *Close-up photo of serious man with scar on his face* [Image]. Pexels. https://www.pexels.com/photo/close-up-photo-of-serious-man-with-scar-on-his-face-7265997/

Green, A. (2021, February 4). *Multiethnic upset women scolding in room* [Image]. Pexels. https://www.pexels.com/photo/multiethnic-upset-women-scolding-in-room-6382688/

Green, A. (2021, February 4). *Sad lady crying near wall at home* [Image]. Pexels. https://www.pexels.com/photo/sad-lady-crying-near-wall-at-home-6383201/

Green, A. (2021, May 24). *Woman in black tank top and white shorts looking to her left* [Image]. Pexels. https://www.pexels.com/photo/woman-in-black-tank-top-and-white-shorts-looking-to-her-left-7208984/

Holmes, K. (2021, April 23). *Student asking his teacher* [Image]. Pexels. https://www.pexels.com/photo/student-asking-his-teacher-7092583/

Kindel Media. (2020, April 13). *Man in black suit wearing black sunglasses* [Image]. Pexels. https://www.pexels.com/photo/man-in-black-suit-wearing-black-sunglasses-7853824/

Kindel Media. (2021, March 1). *Close-up photography of person in handcuffs* [Image]. Pexels. https://www.pexels.com/photo/close-up-photography-of-person-in-handcuffs-7714892/

Lopes, H. (2018, June 11). *Woman and man wearing brown jackets standing near tree* [Image]. Pexels. https://www.pexels.com/photo/woman-and-man-wearing-brown-jackets-standing-near-tree-984954/

McKinney, D. (2018, August 16). *Man in brown top beside railroad* [Image]. Pexels. https://www.pexels.com/photo/man-in-brown-top-beside-railroad-2432299/

Mentatdgt. (2018, February 14). *Man in black holding phone* [Image]. Pexels. https://www.pexels.com/photo/man-in-black-holding-phone-618613/

Piacquadio, A. (2019, August 18). *Person writing on notebook* [Image]. Pexels. https://www.pexels.com/photo/person-writing-on-notebook-3201466/

RODNAE Productions. (2020, November 9). *Man and woman sitting on counter* [Image]. Pexels. https://www.pexels.com/photo/man-and-woman-sitting-on-counter-4694313/

SHVETS production. (2021, April 30). *Reflection in mirror of young woman* [Image]. Pexels. https://www.pexels.com/photo/reflection-in-mirror-of-young-woman-7678451/

Shvets, A. (2020, November 11). *Woman night relaxation blue* [Image]. Pexels. https://www.pexels.com/photo/woman-night-relaxation-blue-6754018/

Zimmerman, P. (2020, August 12). *Portrait photo of woman in red top wearing black-framed eyeglasses holding out her hand in stop gesture* [Image]. Pexels. https://www.pexels.com/photo/portrait-photo-of-woman-in-red-top-wearing-black-framed-eyeglasses-holding-out-her-hand-in-stop-gesture-3762802/

www.ingramcontent.com/pod-product-compliance
Lightning Source LLC
LaVergne TN
LVHW050935210926
848482LV00013B/624

* 9 7 9 8 9 0 0 1 9 4 3 1 8 *